GORDON
RAMSAY

gordon's
HEALTHY EATING

FOOD BY MARK SARGEANT
TEXT BY EMILY QUAH
PHOTOGRAPHY BY LISA BARBER

 ALHAMBRA
EDITIONS

EDITORIAL DIRECTOR Anne Furniss
CREATIVE DIRECTOR Helen Lewis
EDITOR Janet Illsley
DESIGNER Katherine Keeble
EDITORIAL ASSISTANT Romilly Morgan
PHOTOGRAPHER Lisa Barber
PRODUCTION DIRECTOR Vincent Smith
PRODUCTION CONTROLLER Sasha Taylor

OPTOMEN TELEVISION
MANAGING DIRECTOR Pat Llewellyn
F WORD EXECUTIVE PRODUCERS
Jon Swain and Ben Adler
SERIES PRODUCER Sarah Lazenby
FOOD PRODUCER Sarah Durdin Robertson

Optomen Television Limited
1 Valentine Place
London SE1 8QH
www.optomen.com

First published as *Gordon Ramsay's Healthy
Appetite* in 2008 by Quadrille Publishing Ltd
This edition first published in 2013 by
Alhambra Editions
Alhambra House
27–31 Charing Cross Road
London WC2H 0LS

Text © 2008, 2013 Gordon Ramsay
Photography © 2008 Lisa Barber
Design and layout © 2013
Quadrille Publishing Ltd

Cataloguing in Publication Data: a catalogue
record for this book is available from the
British Library.

ISBN 978 184949 301 7

Printed in China

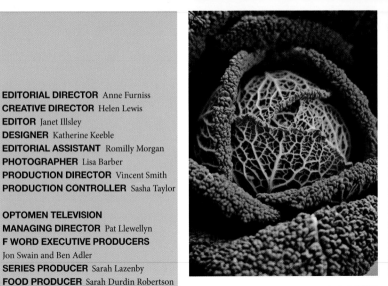

NOTES

All spoon measures are level unless otherwise stated:
1 tsp = 5ml spoon; 1 tbsp = 15ml spoon.

All herbs are fresh, and all pepper is freshly ground black pepper unless otherwise suggested.

I recommend using free-range eggs. If you are pregnant or in a vulnerable health group, avoid those
recipes that contain raw egg whites or lightly cooked eggs.

If possible, buy unwaxed citrus fruit if you are using the zest.

My timings are provided as guidelines, with a description of colour or texture where appropriate.
Oven timings apply to fan-assisted ovens. If using a conventional oven, increase the temperature by
15°C (1 Gas Mark). Use an oven thermometer to check the accuracy of your oven.

Healthy eating is a topic close to my heart. I've been passionate about leading a healthy lifestyle for many years now. It started when I ran the London marathon back in 2000. I was overweight and out-of-shape, but I loved the challenge and now I'm hooked. I've run every London marathon since, even a double marathon in South Africa.

As for maintaining a healthy lifestyle, keeping fit and eating well go hand-in-hand. Any chef will tell you that we lead the most unorthodox and unhealthy lifestyles – we pick at food all day and have no time to exercise. Only on our days off are we likely to eat properly. However, I refuse to be pigeon-holed into a stereotype. With a little extra knowledge and effort, I believe anyone can make small changes that will improve their diet and everyday lifestyle.

Now, let me clarify: this is not a diet book. Those who know me know that I don't believe in faddy diets. I do, however, believe that I can prepare and serve healthy food without jeopardising taste and flavour, or drastically changing my style of cooking. Whether it's an energising breakfast or a simple mid-week supper, a few simple adjustments are all that's needed to make our favourite meals that bit more balanced… lower in fat and calories, yet rich in energy-giving nutrients.

Choosing the right ingredients is the core of healthy eating. It's not just a matter of selecting the leanest cuts of meat and reducing the amount of fat we consume, it helps to know which ingredients are at their peak at any given time, both in terms of flavour and nutrition. Seasonality is very important to me, both at home and in the restaurants.

When it comes to putting a healthy dish together, balance and moderation are key. It's not simply a matter of putting the right types of food on a plate. How the food is cooked and seasoned, and how the whole menu comes together are just as important. And I don't advocate cutting out butter and cream completely, just using a little here and there where it will really enhance the flavour of a dish. After all, a big part of living a good life is the enjoyment of food…

healthy
BREAKFAST

melon &
BERRY SALAD

SERVES 4

Halve the melons, remove and discard the seeds, then use a melon baller to carve out the flesh in balls (or simply cut it into small chunks if you prefer).

Divide the melon balls and mixed berries between individual serving bowls (or simply toss them together in a large salad bowl).

Finely grate the zests from the lime and orange over the fruit salad. Cut the lime and orange in half and squeeze a little juice over each serving. Drizzle with a little honey, then scatter over the mint.

Best served slightly chilled.

1 canteloupe melon
1 honeydew melon
300g mixed berries, such as
   blueberries, blackberries
   and raspberries
1 lime
1 orange
1–2 tsp runny honey
handful of mint leaves, shredded

lightly spiced
DRIED FRUIT COMPOTE

SERVES 4

Put all the dried fruit in a small saucepan with the spices, orange zest and juice, 100ml of water and the liqueur if using. Give the mixture a stir and slowly bring to the boil. Reduce the heat to low and cover the pan with a lid.

Simmer the mixture, giving it an occasional stir, for 8–10 minutes until the fruit is soft and plump and the liquid has reduced and is syrupy. You may need to add a splash of water towards the end if the mixture looks too dry.

Tip into a bowl and leave to cool slightly. Serve in individual bowls with natural or Greek yoghurt.

150g dried prunes
150g dried apricots
100g dried cherries or
    cranberries
100g dried blueberries
1 cinnamon stick
2 star anise
finely grated zest of 1 large
    orange and juice of 2
2 tbsp Grand Marnier (optional)
low-fat natural or Greek yoghurt,
    to serve

porridge

Put the oats, 500ml of water, the milk and salt, if using, into a medium saucepan. Stir well, then place over a high heat until the mixture begins to boil. Reduce the heat to low and stir for 5–8 minutes as the porridge bubbles and thickens. Cook until it is the consistency you like, adding a splash of water if you prefer a thinner porridge.

Take the pan from the heat and divide the porridge between warm bowls. Top each portion with a spoonful of yoghurt, a little honey or brown sugar and a scattering of toasted almonds.

This is also delicious with fresh fruit, or dried fruit compote (see left).

150g porridge oats or medium
   ground oatmeal
500ml semi-skimmed milk
pinch of fine sea salt (optional)

To serve
4 tbsp low-fat natural or
   Greek yoghurt
runny honey or brown sugar
handful of toasted flaked
   almonds

buckwheat pancakes
WITH SMOKED SALMON

Mix the flours, baking powder, salt and sugar together in a large mixing bowl. Make a well in the centre and add the milk and melted butter or oil. Gradually draw the flour mix into the centre, stirring to make a smooth batter. Leave to stand for a few minutes.

When ready to cook, whisk the egg whites in a clean bowl to firm peaks, then fold into the pancake batter. Melt a small knob of butter in each of two non-stick blini pans or one large non-stick frying pan, to lightly coat the base.

Add a small ladleful of batter to each blini pan (or two to the frying pan) and cook over a medium heat for 1½–2 minutes until golden brown on the underside. Flip the pancakes over and cook for another minute. Slide onto a warm plate and keep warm, while you cook the rest of the batter to make 10–12 pancakes in total. (After the first pancake, you probably won't need to add extra butter to the pans.)

Divide the pancakes between warm serving plates and drape a couple of smoked salmon slices around. Drop a spoonful of soured cream in the middle and scatter over the capers and salad leaves, if using. Drizzle with a little olive oil and grind over some black pepper.

85g buckwheat flour
85g plain flour
1½ tsp baking powder
⅓ tsp fine sea salt
1 tbsp caster sugar
200ml semi-skimmed milk
1½ tsp melted butter or light
   olive oil
2 large egg whites
small knob of butter, for cooking

To serve
10–12 slices of sustainably
   sourced smoked salmon
6 tbsp soured cream
3–4 tbsp capers, rinsed
   and drained
handful of salad leaves (optional)
olive oil, to drizzle (optional)
freshly ground black pepper

full english
BREAKFAST

Preheat the grill to the highest setting. Half-fill a wide, shallow pan with water and bring to a simmer. Line a large (or two small) baking sheet(s) with foil, then brush with a little olive oil.

Trim the mushrooms, removing their stalks, then lay, gill sides up, on the baking sheet. Place the vine tomatoes alongside. Drizzle over a little olive oil and sprinkle with a pinch each of salt and pepper. Lay the bacon rashers in a single layer on the baking sheet (the second one if using two). Place under the grill for 5 minutes until the mushrooms are tender and the bacon is golden brown around the edges.

To poach the eggs, break each one into a cup or ramekin. Add a dash of vinegar to the pan of simmering water. Whisk the water in a circular motion to create a whirlpool effect. Gently slide the eggs into the centre of the whirlpool, one at a time, then reduce the heat to a low simmer. Poach for 1½ minutes if the eggs were at room temperature, or 2 minutes if they were straight from the fridge. The whites will have set but the yolks should still be runny in the middle.

Divide the bacon, mushrooms, tomatoes and rye toasts between warm serving plates. Carefully lift out each poached egg with a slotted spoon, dab the bottom of the spoon with kitchen paper to absorb any excess water and slide onto a rye toast. Grind some pepper over the eggs and serve at once.

olive oil, to brush and drizzle
4 portabello mushrooms, cleaned
300g vine-ripened cherry
    tomatoes
sea salt and black pepper
16 rashers of smoked back bacon
8 large eggs
dash of white-wine vinegar
8 slices of rye bread, toasted

herb omelette with
CHERRY TOMATOES

SERVES 1

Halve the cherry tomatoes or cut into quarters. Heat the olive oil in a non-stick omelette pan and tip in the tomatoes. Season with salt and pepper and fry over a medium heat for 1–2 minutes until the tomatoes are just soft but still retaining their shape.

Meanwhile, lightly beat the eggs in a bowl. Scatter the chopped herbs over the tomatoes, then pour in the beaten eggs. Quickly stir and shake the pan to distribute the eggs and ensure they cook evenly. When they are almost set, take the pan off the heat.

Fold the omelette, using a heatproof spatula to lift one edge and tipping the pan slightly to make it easier to fold over. Slide onto a warm plate and serve immediately.

8–10 cherry tomatoes
1 tbsp olive oil
sea salt and black pepper
3 large eggs
handful of mixed herb leaves, such as flat leaf parsley, chives and chervil, chopped

scrambled egg, anchovy
& ASPARAGUS

SERVES 4

To prepare the asparagus, snap off the woody base of the stalks. Bring a pan of salted water to the boil and blanch the asparagus spears for 3–4 minutes or until tender. Meanwhile, chop 2 anchovies very finely.

Break the eggs into a cold, heavy-based pan and add a knob of butter and the chopped anchovies. Place the pan on the lowest heat possible and, using a heatproof spatula, stir the eggs vigorously to begin with to combine the yolks with the whites, then intermittently but frequently.

As the eggs begin to set, add a little salt, some pepper and the chopped basil. They will take about 4 minutes to scramble and you might need to keep moving the pan on and off the heat so that they don't get overheated. The scrambled eggs should still be soft and creamy.

Drain the asparagus as soon as it is ready and dab dry with kitchen paper. Divide between warm serving plates. Pile the scrambled eggs on top and drape a few anchovy fillets over each serving. If you wish, drizzle a little olive oil around the plate. Serve immediately.

250g asparagus spears
sea salt and black pepper
100g marinated fresh anchovy
   fillets (available in tubs from
   delis and good supermarkets)
10 large free-range eggs
knob of butter
4 large basil leaves, roughly
   chopped
a little olive oil, to drizzle
   (optional)

ricotta & walnut
BAKED MUSHROOMS

SERVES 4

Heat the oven to 200°C/Gas 6. Line a large baking sheet with foil and brush with a little olive oil. Place the mushrooms, gill sides up, on the baking sheet. Sprinkle with a small pinch each of salt and pepper.

In a bowl, mix together the ricotta, walnuts, oregano, Parmesan and a little seasoning. Spread a teaspoonful of the mixture on top of each mushroom, then drizzle over a little olive oil. Bake for 10 minutes until the mushrooms are tender.

Lightly toast the bread in the meantime. Place a couple of slices on each warm serving plate and arrange the mushrooms on top. Drizzle with a little olive oil if you like and serve warm.

olive oil, to drizzle
300g portabellini (baby portabello) mushrooms, cleaned
sea salt and black pepper
350g ricotta
60g (about 4 tbsp) chopped walnuts
1 oregano sprig, leaves only, chopped
2 tbsp grated Parmesan
8 slices of multi-seeded rye or sourdough bread

berry & yoghurt
SMOOTHIE

SERVES 4–6

Place all the ingredients in a blender and whizz until smooth, sweetening the mixture with icing sugar or maple syrup to taste. Serve in chilled glasses.

200g raspberries
200g blackberries
6 heaped tbsp low-fat natural yoghurt
300ml milk
3–4 tbsp icing sugar or maple syrup, to taste

more ideas
FOR SMOOTHIES...

FIG, HONEY AND YOGHURT

Trim 8 ripe figs, removing the tops, then cut into quarters. Put into a blender along with 600ml semi-skimmed milk, 200ml low-fat natural yoghurt and 6–8 tbsp honey to taste. Add 4–6 ice cubes for extra chill, if you like. Blend until smooth and thick, then pour into chilled glasses. Serves 4

POMEGRANATE AND BANANA

Peel 3 large ripe bananas, cut into chunks and freeze in a plastic bag for an hour. Drop the banana chunks into a blender. Scrape the seeds from a vanilla pod with the back of a knife and add them to the blender. Pour in 250ml pomegranate juice, 500ml low-fat natural yoghurt and 1–2 tbsp honey. Blend until smooth and serve in chilled glasses. Serves 4

wholemeal
BLUEBERRY MUFFINS

MAKES 12

Heat the oven to 180°C/Gas 4. Line a 12-hole muffin tin with muffin cases. Peel the bananas and mash in a bowl, using a fork.

Mix the flour, baking powder, bicarbonate of soda, salt and brown sugar together in a large mixing bowl. Make a well in the centre and add the buttermilk, egg, olive oil and bananas. Quickly fold the ingredients together until just incorporated, taking care not to overmix. Tip in the blueberries and give the batter one or two stirs.

Spoon the batter into the muffin cases and sprinkle with the demerara sugar. The cases will be quite full. Bake in the oven for 20–25 minutes until well risen and golden brown on top; a skewer inserted into the centre of the muffin should emerge clean.

Leave to cool in the tin for a couple of minutes, then transfer to a wire rack to cool completely.

2 very ripe large bananas
300g wholemeal flour
1½ tsp baking powder
1 tsp bicarbonate of soda
pinch of fine sea salt
100g light muscovado or
   brown sugar
284ml carton buttermilk
1 large egg, lightly beaten
75g light olive oil (or
   melted butter)
200g blueberries, rinsed
   and drained
1 tbsp demerara sugar

healthy
BRUNCH

cod & tomato
CHOWDER

SERVES 4–5

Heat the olive oil in a heavy-based pan. Add the onions, celery and some seasoning, and stir over a medium heat for 6–8 minutes to soften. Add the carrots, potatoes, yellow pepper and herbs, and sauté for 5 minutes until the vegetables are lightly golden.

Add the tomatoes to the pan and pour in the stock. Cover and simmer for 7–9 minutes until the vegetables are tender. Now tip in the French beans and courgettes, give the mixture a stir and simmer for another 3 minutes. Check the seasoning, adding a few dashes of Tabasco to spice up the chowder if you like.

Lightly season the cod fillets and lay them on the vegetables in the pan. Cover the pan again and simmer for 3–4 minutes until the fish is opaque and just cooked through.

Using a spoon, gently break the fish into large flakes. Ladle the hot soup into warm bowls and scatter a handful of chopped parsley over each serving.

3 tbsp olive oil
2 medium onions, peeled and
    roughly chopped
2 celery sticks, trimmed and
    roughly chopped
sea salt and black pepper
2 large carrots, peeled and
    roughly chopped
2 large waxy potatoes,
    about 400g, peeled and
    roughly chopped
1 yellow pepper, cored, deseeded
    and roughly chopped
few thyme sprigs
1 bay leaf
400g can chopped tomatoes
900ml fish or chicken stock
    (see pages 154–5)
150g French beans, cut into
    short lengths
2 courgettes, roughly chopped
few dashes of Tabasco sauce
    (optional)
600g sustainably sourced cod
    fillets, skinned and pin-boned
bunch of flat leaf parsley, leaves
    only, roughly chopped

persian-style
ONION SOUP

SERVES 4

Place a heavy-based pan over a medium heat. Add 2 tbsp olive oil, the onions and some seasoning. Cover and sweat for 12–15 minutes until the onions are soft, lifting the lid and stirring occasionally. Remove the lid and increase the heat very slightly.

Add the spices, dried mint and remaining oil, then stir in the flour. Cook, stirring frequently, for 3–4 minutes. Gradually pour in the stock, whisking as you do so to prevent any lumps forming. When it has all been added, drop in the cinnamon stick and simmer over a low heat, partially covered with the lid, for 30–40 minutes.

Stir in the lemon juice and sugar, then taste and adjust the seasoning. Discard the cinnamon stick. Ladle the soup into warm bowls and scatter over the parsley to serve.

3 tbsp olive oil
5 large onions, peeled and
   thinly sliced
sea salt and black pepper
½ tsp ground turmeric
½ tsp fenugreek seeds
½ tsp dried mint
2 tbsp plain flour
700ml vegetable or chicken stock
   (see pages 154–5)
1 cinnamon stick
juice of 1 lemon
1 tsp caster sugar
few flat leaf parsley leaves,
   chopped

smoked trout, orange
& WILD ROCKET SALAD

To segment the oranges, cut off the top and bottom of one and stand it upright on a board. Cut along the curve of the fruit to remove the skin and white pith, exposing the flesh. Now hold the orange over a sieve set on top of a bowl and cut out the segments between the membranes, letting each one drop into the sieve as you go along. Finally, squeeze the membrane over the sieve to extract as much juice as possible. Repeat with the remaining oranges, then tip all the segments into another bowl.

For the dressing, add the olive oil and a little seasoning to the orange juice that you've collected in the bowl and whisk to combine.

Add the rocket to the orange segments, then flake the smoked trout into the bowl. Add the dressing and toss gently with your hands. Pile onto individual plates and serve with pumpernickel or rye bread.

3 oranges
4 tbsp extra virgin olive oil,
    to drizzle
sea salt and black pepper
200g wild rocket leaves, washed
2 sustainably sourced
    hot-smoked trout fillets,
    about 125g each

devilled caesar salad
WITH PARMA HAM

SERVES 4

To make the dressing, whizz all the ingredients together in a food processor, seasoning with pepper to taste. You'll probably find that the anchovies provide enough salt.

Cook the Parma ham in two batches. Heat a tiny drizzle of olive oil in a non-stick frying pan and lay in half the ham slices. Fry over a medium heat for a couple of minutes on each side until golden brown, then transfer to a plate. Cook the rest in the same way. Leave until cool and crisp, then break the Parma ham slices into smaller pieces.

Lightly toast the ciabatta slices in the same pan, turning to colour both sides. Remove and cut into chunky croûtons. Separate the lettuce leaves and divide between serving plates. Scatter over the croûtons, Parma ham and anchovies. Drizzle over the dressing and scatter with Parmesan shavings to serve.

8 slices of Parma ham
a little olive oil
8 thick slices of ciabatta
4 baby gem lettuce, trimmed
    and washed
15–16 (about 60g) marinated
    fresh anchovy fillets
Parmesan shavings, to finish

For the dressing
1 garlic clove, peeled and crushed
2 salted anchovies, rinsed,
    drained and finely chopped
½ tsp paprika
few dashes of Worcestershire
    sauce
100g natural or Greek yoghurt
freshly ground black pepper

warm ham hocks with
WILD RICE & BASMATI

SERVES 4

Put the ham hocks into a large pan with the onion, carrot, celery, herbs and peppercorns. Pour over enough cold water to cover the hocks and bring to the boil, then skim off any scum from the surface. Cover and simmer gently for 3–4 hours until the hocks are very tender – the meat should slide easily from the bone.

Leave the hocks to cool slightly in the poaching stock, then lift onto a plate. While still warm, peel off the skin and remove the fat. Break the meat into flakes and place in a salad bowl.

Measure 1 litre of the ham poaching stock. (You can save the rest to make a soup.) Pour the measured stock into a medium saucepan and add the basmati and wild rice. Bring to the boil, lower the heat to a simmer and cook for 20–25 minutes until the rice is tender.

Meanwhile, blanch the French beans: add them to a pan of boiling salted water and cook for 3–4 minutes until just tender. Drain and refresh under cold running water. Drain thoroughly.

Drain the rice in a colander set over another pan. Place the pan lid over the colander to let the rice steam and dry out a little, then tip into the bowl containing the ham. Add the beans, parsley, lemon juice, olive oil and a generous grinding of black pepper. Toss well and serve warm, or at room temperature if you prefer.

For the ham hocks
2 smoked ham hocks, about
   800g each, soaked overnight
   and drained
1 onion, peeled and halved
1 large carrot, peeled and cut into
   3 chunks
1 celery stick, trimmed and cut
   into 3 pieces
handful of flat leaf parsley sprigs
handful of thyme sprigs
1 bay leaf
½ tsp black peppercorns

For the rice and salad
150g mixed basmati and wild rice
150g French beans, trimmed
   and halved
handful of flat leaf parsley leaves,
   roughly torn
squeeze of lemon juice, to taste
3 tbsp extra virgin olive oil
freshly ground black pepper

sweet potato frittata
WITH TOMATO SALSA

To make the salsa, halve or quarter the tomatoes and place in a large bowl. Add all the other ingredients and mix well, seasoning to taste with salt and pepper, and a pinch of sugar if you like. Set aside.

For the frittata, heat the grill to its highest setting. Peel the sweet potato and cut into 1cm cubes. Heat a non-stick omelette or frying pan (suitable for use under the grill) and add the olive oil. When hot, toss in the potato and shallot, and season well with salt and pepper. Cook over a medium heat, turning occasionally, for 4–5 minutes until the sweet potatoes are just tender and lightly golden at the edges.

Lightly beat the eggs in a bowl, add the chives and pour over the sweet potatoes. Shake the pan gently to distribute the ingredients and cook over a low heat, without stirring, for a few minutes until the eggs are beginning to set at the bottom and around the sides.

Place the pan under the hot grill briefly until the top of the frittata has set. Try not to overcook the eggs or they will turn rubbery. Leave to stand for a minute, then run a heatproof plastic spatula around the sides of the pan and invert the frittata onto a large plate. Spoon the tomato salsa into a neat pile on top and serve immediately.

1 large sweet potato, 200–250g
1 tbsp olive oil
1 shallot, peeled and finely
   chopped
sea salt and black pepper
4 large eggs
small handful of chives, snipped

For the tomato salsa
250g vine-ripened plum
   tomatoes
2 spring onions, trimmed and
   thinly sliced on the diagonal
handful of coriander leaves,
   chopped
juice of ½ lemon
3 tbsp extra virgin olive oil
1 tbsp sesame oil
dash of Tabasco sauce
pinch of caster sugar (optional)

spinach &
GOAT'S CHEESE SOUFFLÉ

SERVES 8

Heat the oven to 200°C/Gas 6. Brush 8 ramekins, each 150ml capacity, with very soft butter, using upward strokes. Set them on a baking tray, chill for 15 minutes, then repeat with another coating of butter.

Set a large pan over a medium-high heat. When hot, add the spinach and some seasoning. Stir for a few minutes until the leaves have wilted, adding a tiny splash of water as necessary. Tip into a colander set over a large bowl. Cool slightly, then wrap the spinach in a clean tea towel and squeeze out the excess moisture. Chop finely and set aside.

Heat the olive oil in a medium saucepan and add the shallot and garlic. Stir over a medium heat for 4–6 minutes until soft. Add the flour and cayenne pepper and stir over a low heat for 3–4 minutes. Gradually whisk in the milk. Simmer and stir for a few more minutes until the mixture thickens. Transfer to a large bowl and cool slightly.

Crumble the goat's cheese into the mixture, then add the Parmesan and a little seasoning and stir to combine. Mix in the chopped spinach and egg yolks. Set aside.

Beat the egg whites in a clean bowl with an electric whisk to firm peaks, then fold into the spinach and cheese mixture until just combined. Spoon into the prepared ramekins and tap gently on the work surface to get rid of any large air pockets. Run the tip of a small knife around the edge of each one. Bake for 13–15 minutes until risen and golden brown on top. Serve immediately, with a simple side salad.

softened butter, for the dishes
500g baby leaf spinach, washed
sea salt and black pepper
3 tbsp olive oil (or butter)
1 banana shallot, peeled and
   finely chopped
2 garlic cloves, peeled
   and crushed
40g plain flour
pinch of cayenne pepper,
   or to taste
250ml semi-skimmed milk
200g soft goat's cheese
2 tbsp finely grated Parmesan
4 large eggs, separated

spaghetti
VONGOLE

Scrub the clams under cold running water and discard any that do not close tightly when gently tapped on the work surface. Meanwhile, bring a large pan of salted water to the boil for the pasta. When it comes to a rolling boil, add the spaghetti and cook until al dente.

Cook the clams about 6 minutes before the pasta will be ready: heat another large pan and add the olive oil. Tip in the clams and throw in the garlic, shallot, chilli and basil stalks. Pour in the wine and cover the pan with a tight-fitting lid. Shake the pan and leave to steam for 3–4 minutes until the clams have opened. Tip the clams into a colander set over a large clean bowl. Discard any that have not opened.

Pour the clam juices back into the pan and boil for a few minutes until thickened slightly. Throw in the parsley, then taste and adjust the seasoning. Clams are naturally salty so you may only need pepper.

Drain the pasta thoroughly. Immediately add to the sauce and toss to coat. Return the clams to the pan and toss again. Divide between warm plates and serve immediately, with chunks of crusty bread to mop up the juices.

2kg fresh palourdes (carpet shell clams) in the shell
sea salt and black pepper
300g dried spaghetti or linguine
2 tbsp olive oil
3 fat garlic cloves, peeled
1 banana shallot, peeled and roughly sliced
1 small red chilli, quartered lengthways
handful of basil stalks
75ml dry white wine
2 tbsp finely chopped flat leaf parsley leaves

soba noodle soup with
CHICKEN & SHIITAKE

SERVES 4

First, marinate the chicken. Cut the chicken breasts across the grain into thin slices. Place in a bowl and add the tamari, mirin, sake, sesame oil and a generous grinding of pepper. Give the chicken a good stir, to ensure that every piece is coated. Cover with cling film and leave in the fridge for at least 30 minutes, or preferably overnight.

For the soup base, pour the chicken stock into a medium pan and add the kombu. Bring to a simmer, cover the pan with a lid and cook gently for 5–10 minutes. Fish out and discard the kombu, which will have imparted a lovely savoury flavour to the stock. Add the ginger and stir in the miso paste. Simmer for another 3–5 minutes.

When ready to serve, bring a pot of water to the boil for the noodles. Add the mushrooms to the simmering stock and cook for 2 minutes, then add the chicken strips. Cook until the chicken is just opaque throughout, about 1–1½ minutes. Taste and adjust the seasoning. Cover the pan with a lid and reduce the heat to as low as possible.

Add the noodles to the pan of boiling water and cook until tender but still retaining a slight bite, about 3–4 minutes. Drain and immediately toss with a little sesame oil. Divide between warm soup bowls and scatter over the spring onions. Ladle the hot soup over the noodles, making sure that you divide the chicken and mushrooms evenly. Sprinkle with the sesame seeds and serve at once.

2 large boneless, skinless chicken breasts, about 150g each
1 tbsp tamari or light soy sauce
2 tbsp mirin
1 tbsp sake
1 tbsp sesame oil, plus more for the noodles
freshly ground black pepper
1.5 litres chicken stock (see page 155)
1 piece of kombu (Japanese dried kelp), rinsed
3cm knob of fresh root ginger, peeled and cut into matchsticks
2–3 tbsp miso paste
200g soba noodles (Japanese buckwheat noodles)
150g shiitake mushrooms, stems trimmed and top scored
4 spring onions, trimmed and thinly sliced on the diagonal
1 tsp toasted sesame seeds

healthy
WEEKDAY LUNCH

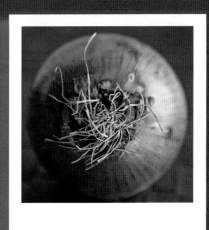

borscht

SERVES 4

Heat the olive oil in a large pan and add the onion, celery, carrot, thyme leaves and some seasoning. Cook over a medium heat, stirring frequently, for 8–10 minutes.

Add the beetroot and cabbage with a small splash of water. Stir well, then cover and cook for 10–12 minutes, stirring several times during cooking to make sure the vegetables do not catch and burn, until the vegetables are just tender.

Remove the lid and pour in the stock or water to cover the vegetables. Add the vinegar, bring to the boil, then reduce the heat to a simmer. Cook for another 5–10 minutes until the vegetables are soft. Skim off any froth from the surface. Adjust the seasoning to taste with salt, pepper and sugar.

Purée the soup with a stick blender until smooth and creamy, or leave it chunky for a traditional, rustic finish. (If you decide to purée the soup, you may need to thin it down slightly with a little boiling water.)

Ladle into warm bowls if serving hot; otherwise allow to cool, then chill thoroughly. Serve topped with the chopped dill and a dollop of soured cream if you like.

2 tbsp olive oil

1 onion, peeled and finely chopped

2 celery sticks, trimmed and finely chopped

1 large carrot, peeled and finely chopped

1 thyme sprig, leaves stripped

sea salt and black pepper

500g raw beetroot, peeled and chopped

¼ red cabbage, about 250g, finely chopped

800ml vegetable stock (see page 154), or water

1 tbsp red-wine vinegar, to taste

1 tsp caster sugar, to taste

handful of dill fronds, chopped

4 tbsp soured cream, or natural yoghurt, to serve (optional)

chilled watercress
& SPINACH SOUP

SERVES 4

Heat the olive oil in a large saucepan and add the onion and potato. Sauté gently, stirring frequently, for about 10 minutes until the vegetables are soft but not brown.

Add the watercress and spinach, then pour in enough stock to cover the vegetables. Bring to the boil and season to taste with salt, pepper and lemon juice. As soon as the spinach and watercress have wilted, remove the pan from the heat.

Purée the soup in two batches, using a blender. Pour into a wide bowl and leave to cool completely. Cover with cling film and chill for a few hours or overnight.

To serve, pour the soup into chilled bowls and garnish with a few baby spinach leaves. Add a small dollop of crème fraîche if you wish, and grind over some pepper.

2 tbsp olive oil
1 sweet onion, peeled and
   finely chopped
1 small potato, about 150g,
   peeled and diced
300g watercress, washed and
   thicker stalks removed
75–100g baby spinach leaves,
   plus a handful to garnish
800ml vegetable or chicken stock
   (see pages 154–5)
sea salt and black pepper
squeeze of lemon juice
3–4 tbsp crème fraîche, to serve
   (optional)

borlotti bean
MINESTRONE

Heat the olive oil in a large pan and add the onions, carrots, celery and some seasoning. Stir frequently over a medium-high heat for 6–8 minutes until the vegetables are beginning to soften. Add the thyme, bay leaf and bacon. Increase the heat slightly and cook, stirring, for another 2 minutes.

Stir in the tomato purée and cook for another minute. Tip in the borlotti beans and cherry tomatoes, then pour in the stock or water to cover. Bring to a gentle simmer. Add the spaghetti and cook for 10 minutes. Taste and adjust the seasoning.

Ladle into warm soup bowls and scatter over the shredded basil. If you wish, add a restrained drizzle of olive oil and grate a little Parmesan over each portion. Serve with chunks of rustic country bread.

2 tbsp olive oil, plus more to
   serve (optional)
2 onions, peeled and chopped
2 carrots, peeled and chopped
1 celery stick, trimmed
   and chopped
sea salt and black pepper
few thyme sprigs
1 bay leaf
80g smoked back bacon,
   trimmed of fat and chopped
2 tbsp tomato purée
2 x 400g cans borlotti beans,
   drained and rinsed
150g cherry tomatoes, halved
600–800ml chicken stock
   (see page 155) or water
75g spaghetti, broken into pieces
large handful of basil leaves,
   shredded
Parmesan, to serve (optional)

thai rice noodle salad
WITH PRAWNS

SERVES 2–3

Bring the kettle to the boil. Place the rice noodles in a large heatproof bowl and pour on boiling water, ensuring that the noodles are fully immersed. Cover with cling film and leave to stand for 5 minutes or until the noodles are tender but still retaining a bite. Drain and toss with a drizzle of sesame oil to stop them sticking to each other.

In the meantime, blanch the mangetout in a pan of boiling water for 2 minutes until they are just tender but still bright green. Refresh in a bowl of iced water, then drain well. Cut them on the diagonal into 2 or 3 pieces. Halve, core and deseed the peppers, then cut into long, thin slices. Trim and finely slice the spring onions on the diagonal.

For the dressing, put all the ingredients into a bowl and whisk lightly.

Put the prawns, spring onions, mangetout and peppers into a large bowl and add the drained noodles, coriander leaves and sesame seeds. Pour the dressing over the salad and toss well to coat. Eat immediately or chill until ready to serve.

NOTE If you're preparing this salad for a packed lunch, leave the noodles to cool completely before tossing with the other ingredients.

100g thin rice noodles

drizzle of sesame oil

200g mangetout or sugar snap peas

1 large red pepper

1 large yellow or orange pepper

2 spring onions

200g sustainably sourced peeled, cooked prawns, deveined if necessary

handful of coriander leaves

1 tbsp toasted black or white sesame seeds

For the dressing

1 shallot, peeled and finely diced

2 garlic cloves, peeled and crushed

1 small red chilli, deseeded and finely chopped

2–3 tbsp lime juice, or more to taste

2 tbsp fish sauce

1 tbsp light soy sauce

2½ tbsp palm sugar or soft brown sugar

2 tbsp toasted sesame oil

flatbread, feta &
CHICKPEA SALAD

SERVES 3–4

Heat the oven to 180°C/Gas 4. Split the breads horizontally. Mix the paprika with 2 tbsp of the olive oil. Brush each piece of bread with this mixture and place on a baking sheet. Bake until lightly golden brown and crisp, just 2–3 minutes for thin flatbreads, 4–5 minutes for pittas.

Meanwhile, heat the remaining olive oil in a pan, add the onion and cook, stirring, over a medium heat for 6–8 minutes until soft. Add the garlic and chilli and fry for another minute. Tip in the chickpeas and stir to mix. Squeeze over the lemon juice and add the parsley and a little seasoning to taste. Warm the chickpeas through, then tip into a large bowl and leave to stand for a few minutes.

Crumble two-thirds of the cheese over the chickpea mixture and toss well. Divide between serving plates and crumble over the remaining feta. Break the bread into smaller pieces and serve on the side.

NOTE If you're preparing this salad for a packed lunch, leave the chickpea mixture to cool completely before adding the feta. Pack the bread in a separate airtight container to keep it crisp.

2 large, thin flatbreads or pittas
½ tsp paprika
4 tbsp olive oil
1 red onion, peeled and
    thinly sliced
2 garlic cloves, peeled and
    thinly sliced
½ red chilli, deseeded and
    finely chopped
400g can chickpeas, drained
    and rinsed
generous squeeze of lemon juice
large handful of flat leaf parsley
    leaves
sea salt and black pepper
150g feta cheese

creole-spiced beans
& VEGETABLES

SERVES 6

Heat the olive oil in a pan and add the onion with some salt and pepper. Stir frequently over a medium heat for 6–8 minutes until the onion is soft.

Meanwhile, combine the ingredients for the Creole spice mix in a small bowl. Add to the pan and stir for a minute or two until fragrant.

Tip the French beans, courgettes and spring onions into the pan and cook for 6–8 minutes until tender. Turn off the heat, add the canned beans and chickpeas along with the cherry tomatoes, and toss to mix.

Transfer the salad to a large bowl and stir in the parsley and coriander. Serve slightly warm or at room temperature.

2 tbsp olive oil
1 onion, peeled and thinly sliced
sea salt and black pepper
200g French beans, trimmed
2 courgettes, trimmed and sliced
    into 1½cm rounds
8 spring onions, trimmed and cut
    into short lengths
400g can haricot or butterbeans,
    drained and rinsed
400g can cannellini beans,
    drained and rinsed
400g can chickpeas, drained
    and rinsed
250g cherry tomatoes, halved
bunch of flat-leaf parsley, leaves
    only, roughly chopped
bunch of coriander, leaves only,
    roughly chopped

For the Creole spice mix
1½ tsp sweet paprika
1½ tsp dried basil
1½ tsp dried thyme
pinch of cayenne pepper,
    or to taste
pinch of chilli powder,
    or to taste

glazed salmon with
SPINACH-RADISH SALAD

SERVES 4

Remove the skin from the salmon and check carefully for pin-bones, pulling out any with kitchen tweezers. Place the fillets side by side in a shallow dish. For the marinade, mix the ingredients in a bowl, then pour over the salmon to coat. Cover with cling film and leave in the fridge for 30 minutes to allow the flavours to permeate. Return the fish to room temperature before continuing.

For the dressing, whisk all the ingredients in a bowl and set aside.

Heat the oven to 230°C/Gas 8. Arrange the spinach leaves on individual plates and top with the radish slices.

Lift the salmon from the marinade and arrange on a lightly oiled baking tray. Cook in the oven for 4–6 minutes until medium rare, basting after 2 minutes. It should feel slightly springy when pressed.

Place a salmon fillet in the middle of each plate and drizzle the ginger and tahini dressing over the salad to serve.

NOTE If you're preparing this salad for a packed lunch, allow the salmon to cool and pack the dressing and salad in separate containers. Assemble just before eating.

4 sustainably sourced lightly smoked salmon fillets, 125–150g each
100g baby spinach leaves, washed and dried
8–10 radishes, washed, trimmed and finely sliced

For the marinade
3 tbsp honey
1 tbsp lemon juice
2 tbsp light soy sauce
1 tsp Dijon mustard
½ tsp grated fresh root ginger

For the dressing
1 tbsp grated fresh root ginger
3 tbsp rice-wine vinegar
2 tbsp light soy sauce
2 tbsp sesame oil
2–3 tbsp tahini

mango, avocado &
SMOKED CHICKEN SALAD

SERVES 4

Peel the mangoes and cut the flesh away from the stone into thin slices. Arrange on four serving plates.

Halve the avocados and remove the stone. Peel off the skin and slice the flesh into strips. Squeeze over a little lemon juice to stop the flesh discolouring, then arrange over the mango slices.

Cut the chicken into thin slices and divide between the plates. Neatly pile the salad leaves in the middle.

For the dressing, whisk the ingredients together in a bowl, seasoning with salt and pepper to taste. Spoon the dressing over the salad and serve, topped with a handful of toasted pine nuts if you like.

NOTE If you're preparing this salad for a packed lunch, pack the dressing and salad in separate containers and mix just before eating.

2 medium, ripe-but-firm mangoes
2 ripe avocados
squeeze of lemon juice
300–350g smoked chicken breasts
200g mixed salad leaves, such
    as rocket, mâche, baby chard
    or amaranth
2 tbsp pine nuts, toasted (optional)

For the dressing
2 tbsp orange juice
2 tbsp lemon juice
1 tbsp wholegrain mustard
2 tbsp extra virgin olive oil
2 tbsp avocado oil (or more
    olive oil)
sea salt and black pepper

healthy
SUNDAY LUNCH

baked sea bass
WITH LEMON COUSCOUS

SERVES 4

Heat the oven to 200°C/Gas 6. Score the sea bass on both sides and rub all over with salt, pepper and a little drizzle of olive oil. Roll a large basil leaf tightly around each rosemary sprig. Insert into the slashes in the fish, along with the garlic slices.

Lay the sea bass on a lightly oiled foil-lined baking tray. Stuff the cavity with the lemon wedges and remaining rosemary. Bake for 15–20 minutes until the flesh is opaque and just cooked through; you should be able to pull out a fin easily.

Prepare the couscous while the fish is in the oven. Put the couscous, lemon zest, chopped rosemary and some seasoning into a large bowl and pour over the boiling water or stock. Cover with cling film and leave for 5 minutes. Meanwhile, cook the peas in boiling water for 3–4 minutes until tender.

For the dressing, mix the lemon juice with the extra virgin olive oil and some seasoning to taste. Once the couscous has absorbed all the stock or water, fluff it up with a fork. Drain the peas and add to the couscous along with the dressing and chopped parsley. Toss to mix.

Serve the fish with the couscous and steamed pak choi or green beans.

NOTE To serve eight, cook two sea bass of this size rather than a larger fish, and make double the quantity of couscous.

1 sustainably sourced sea bass, about 1.1kg, scaled and gutted
sea salt and black pepper
olive oil, to drizzle
handful of large basil leaves
few tender rosemary sprigs
2 large garlic cloves, peeled and thinly sliced
½ lemon, cut into wedges

For the couscous
250g couscous
finely grated zest of 1 lemon
1 tender rosemary sprig, needles stripped and finely chopped
300ml boiling water or chicken stock (see page 155)
250g peas, thawed if frozen
juice of ½ lemon
4 tbsp extra virgin olive oil
bunch of flat leaf parsley, leaves only, chopped

marinated halibut with
SPICED AUBERGINES

SERVES 4

Lay the fish in a shallow dish and drizzle over the olive oil. Sprinkle with pepper and the turmeric, and rub all over to coat evenly. Cover with cling film and leave to marinate in the fridge for a few hours, or for at least 20 minutes.

Heat the oven to 200°C/Gas 6. Cut the aubergines into 3cm chunks, sprinkle with salt and leave to stand in a colander set over a bowl for 20 minutes. (Doing this prevents them from absorbing as much oil during cooking.)

Rinse the aubergines to remove the salt, drain well and pat dry with kitchen paper. Toss them in a large baking tray with some black pepper and 2–3 tbsp olive oil. Bake for 20–25 minutes until the aubergines are soft.

Meanwhile, heat the remaining olive oil in a pan. Add the onions with some seasoning and sweat over a medium heat for 8–10 minutes until soft. Add the cumin and fry for a few more minutes until the onions are lightly caramelised. Take off the heat. When the aubergines are ready, add them to the onions with the tomatoes, sultanas, lemon juice and salt and pepper to taste.

To cook the fish, heat a large non-stick frying pan and fry the fish fillets for 2 minutes on each side; they should feel just firm when lightly pressed. Leave to rest for a minute or two while you reheat the spiced aubergines. Pile these onto warm plates and top with the halibut fillets. Scatter the basil around and drizzle over a little turmeric oil from the pan.

6 sustainably sourced skinless
   halibut fillets, about 130g each
3 tbsp olive oil
sea salt and black pepper
¾ tsp ground turmeric

For the spiced aubergines
3 large aubergines
5 tbsp olive oil
3 large onions, peeled and
   finely sliced
2 tsp ground cumin
3 plum tomatoes, skinned,
   deseeded and chopped
150g sultanas, soaked in hot
   water for 10 minutes
2–3 tbsp lemon juice, to taste
handful of basil leaves, torn

roast chicken
WITH BABY VEGETABLES

SERVES 4–6

Heat the oven to 230°C/Gas 8. Rub the chicken all over with salt, pepper and a little drizzle of olive oil. Place in a large roasting pan and stuff the cavity with half the head of garlic, 2 or 3 lemon halves and a few herb sprigs.

Roast the chicken for 20 minutes, then take it out of the oven and lower the setting to 200°C/Gas 6. Add the carrots and turnips to the roasting pan and turn to baste in the juices. Put the remaining garlic, lemon halves and herbs around the chicken. Drizzle a little olive oil over the bird and vegetables, and sprinkle with a little salt and pepper. Roast for another 35–40 minutes or until the bird is golden brown and cooked through; the juices should run clear when the thickest part of the thigh is pierced with a knife.

When ready, lift the chicken onto a warm platter, cover with foil and leave to rest for 10–15 minutes in a warm place. Put the vegetables into a warm dish, cover and keep hot.

Meanwhile, skim off any fat from the cooking juices in the roasting pan, then place on the hob over a medium heat. Add the wine, scraping up the sediment from the bottom of the tray to deglaze and let bubble until reduced by half. Pour in the stock and again boil until reduced by half. Add any juices from the rested chicken, then strain into a warm jug.

Carve the chicken and divide the meat and roast vegetables between warm plates. Pour the sauce over the chicken. Serve with new potatoes and a green vegetable, such as broccoli or Brussels sprouts.

1 large chicken, 1.8–2kg
sea salt and black pepper
1 tbsp olive oil, plus a little more
    to drizzle
1 head of garlic, halved
    horizontally
2 lemons, halved
handful of thyme sprigs
few rosemary sprigs
300g baby carrots, scrubbed
300g baby turnips, washed and
    halved if quite large
100ml dry white wine
300ml chicken stock
    (see page 155)

sticky baked
CHICKEN DRUMSTICKS

SERVES 5

Heat the oven to 200°C/Gas 6. Lightly oil a baking dish large enough to hold the chicken in a single layer. Season the drumsticks with salt and pepper and arrange in the dish. Drizzle over a little olive oil and bake in the hot oven for 20 minutes. Meanwhile, prepare the glaze. Mix all the ingredients in a small bowl until combined.

Take the chicken out of the oven and pour over the glaze, turning to coat each drumstick. Return to the oven for another 20–30 minutes, turning several times, until the chicken is tender and nicely glazed.

Let the chicken rest for a few minutes. For a balanced meal, serve with steamed rice and purple-sprouting broccoli or green beans.

olive oil, to drizzle
10 chicken drumsticks
sea salt and black pepper

For the glaze
6 tbsp honey
3 tbsp fish sauce
1½ tbsp light soy sauce
juice of 1½ lemons
3 tbsp rice wine vinegar
1½ tbsp sesame oil

pheasant &
GINGER CASSEROLE

Rub the pheasants all over with a little salt and pepper and lay them breast side down in a large cast-iron pan or other flameproof casserole. Add the carrots, celery and onions, along with the ginger, garlic, herbs, cloves, star anise if using, and peppercorns. Pour in enough water to come two-thirds of the way up the sides of the pheasants.

Place over a high heat and bring to the boil. Immediately reduce the heat to a simmer, partially cover the pan with a lid and cook gently for 35–40 minutes until the pheasants are tender, turning them over halfway through cooking.

To serve, lift the pheasants out of the broth and either carve them into smaller joints or remove the meat from the carcass and break into shreds. Divide between warm bowls and ladle over the hot broth and vegetables. Serve with chunks of rustic bread.

2 oven-ready pheasants, about 750g each
sea salt and black pepper
2 large carrots, peeled and each cut into 3 chunks
2 large celery sticks, trimmed and each cut into 3 pieces
200g cipollini or baby onions, peeled
2 x 5cm knobs of fresh root ginger, halved lengthways
1 head of garlic, halved horizontally
handful of thyme sprigs
few rosemary sprigs
5 cloves
2 star anise (optional)
1 tsp black peppercorns

roast fillet of beef,
TOMATO & TARRAGON

SERVES 6

To make the dressing, cut each tomato in half and squeeze out the seeds. Finely chop the flesh and place in a large bowl. Add the rest of the ingredients except for the herbs, and mix well. Season well with salt and pepper to taste. Cover with cling film and chill for at least 20 minutes or until ready to serve.

Heat the oven to 200°C/Gas 6 and preheat a roasting pan. Trim any fat or sinew from the fillet of beef and season all over with salt and pepper. Heat a non-stick frying pan with a little olive oil. When it is very hot, add the beef and sear for 1½–2 minutes on each side until evenly browned all over. Lightly oil the hot roasting pan.

Transfer the beef to the roasting pan and place in the oven. Roast for 25 minutes for medium rare beef; it should feel a little springy when lightly pressed. Place on a warm platter to rest for 10 minutes.

Serve the beef warm or at room temperature. Slice it thickly and overlap the slices on a serving platter. Pile the rocket into the centre. Stir the chopped herbs into the tomato-tarragon dressing and spoon over the beef. Accompany with new potatoes if you like.

1.2kg prime beef fillet (in one piece, cut from the thick end)
sea salt and black pepper
2 tbsp olive oil
few handfuls of wild rocket leaves

For the tomato-tarragon dressing
500g (about 6) ripe plum tomatoes
5 tbsp tomato passata or ketchup, preferably homemade
2 tbsp Worcestershire sauce
1 tbsp Dijon mustard
few dashes of Tabasco sauce
juice of 1 lemon
2 tbsp balsamic vinegar
2 tbsp extra-virgin olive oil
2 shallots, peeled and finely chopped
large handful each of tarragon and flat leaf parsley, chopped

spicy
BEEF CURRY

Cut the beef into bite-sized chunks, put into a bowl and season with salt and pepper. Sprinkle with the garam masala, add the yoghurt and toss to coat. Cover with cling film and leave to marinate in the fridge for at least 30 minutes, or overnight. Remove and set aside to come to room temperature before you start to prepare the curry.

For the spice mix, toast the coriander, cumin, fennel and fenugreek, if using, in a dry pan, tossing over a high heat for a few minutes until the seeds are fragrant. Tip into a mortar, add a pinch of salt and grind to a fine powder. Stir in the curry powder and turmeric.

Heat a film of olive oil in a large cast-iron casserole or a heavy-based pan. Add the onions, garlic, ginger and a little salt and pepper. Stir, then cover and cook for 8–10 minutes until the onions are soft, lifting the lid to give the mixture a stir a few times.

Add a little more oil, tip in the ground spice mix and cook, stirring, for 2 minutes. Add the tomato purée and sugar and stir over a medium-high heat for a few minutes until the onions are lightly caramelised. Add the tomatoes, beef stock, coriander stalks, cardamom pods, curry leaves and whole green chillies.

Add the beef and stir until well coated in the sauce, then partially cover. Simmer very gently, stirring occasionally, for 3–4 hours, depending on the cut of beef, until the meat is meltingly tender.

To serve, ladle the curry into warm bowls and scatter over the coriander leaves. Accompany with a steaming bowl of basmati rice or warmed Indian bread.

2kg good-quality lean braising
  beef or chuck steak
sea salt and black pepper
4 tsp garam masala
4 tbsp natural yoghurt
4–5 tbsp light olive oil
4 large sweet onions, peeled and
  finely chopped
4 garlic cloves, peeled and finely
  chopped
5cm knob of fresh root ginger,
  peeled and finely grated
4 tbsp tomato purée
2 tbsp caster sugar, or to taste
2 x 400g cans chopped tomatoes
800ml beef stock (see page 155)
small handful of coriander,
  leaves separated, stalks
  finely chopped
6–8 cardamom pods
15–20 curry leaves
6 long green chillies

For the spice mix
4 tsp coriander seeds
4 tsp cumin seeds
1 tsp fennel seeds
1 tsp fenugreek seeds (optional)
4 tsp mild curry powder
1 tsp ground turmeric

venison pie with
SWEET POTATO TOPPING

SERVES 4–5

Cut the venison into 2.5–3cm chunks. Season the flour and use to coat the venison. Heat 2 tbsp olive oil in a large flameproof casserole and fry the meat in batches until evenly browned, about 2 minutes each side. Transfer to a bowl and set aside.

Add the leeks, onions and carrots to the casserole with a little more oil and stir over a medium heat for 4–5 minutes until lightly coloured. Add the mushrooms and rosemary and cook for a minute. Pour in the wine, scraping the bottom of the pan with a wooden spoon to deglaze. Bubble until reduced right down.

Pour in the stock and bring to a simmer. Return the venison, with any juices released, to the pan. Partially cover with a lid and gently braise for 40–50 minutes until the venison is tender, stirring occasionally.

About 15 minutes before the venison will be ready, slice the new potatoes into 1cm thick rounds. Season and fry in a little olive oil in a wide non-stick frying pan until golden brown on both sides. Add to the casserole to finish cooking. Once the potatoes and venison are tender, remove the pan from the heat and let cool slightly.

For the topping, peel the potatoes and cut into 5cm chunks. Cook in a pan of salted water for 15 minutes or until tender. Drain well and pass through a potato ricer back into the pan. While hot, mix in the butter, cheese and seasoning. Cool slightly, then mix in the egg yolks.

Heat the oven to 220°C/Gas 7. Tip the venison mixture into a large pie dish or a shallow cast-iron pan and top with the mash. Rough up the surface with a fork. Bake for 20 minutes until the topping is golden brown and the filling bubbling around the sides. Grind over some pepper and serve.

600g haunch of venison
sea salt and black pepper
3 tbsp plain flour
3–4 tbsp olive oil
2 leeks, white part only,
   sliced thickly
150g baby onions, peeled
250g small Chantenay carrots,
   scrubbed
250g chestnut mushrooms,
   halved
1 large rosemary sprig, needles
   only, finely chopped
150ml red wine or port
650ml chicken stock
   (see page 155)
150g new potatoes, scrubbed

For the sweet potato topping
500g sweet potatoes
350g Desirée potatoes
20g butter
50g double Gloucester cheese,
   grated
2 large egg yolks

roast lamb with
PAPRIKA & ORANGES

SERVES 6–8

Heat the oven to 220°C/Gas 7. Trim away any excess fat from the lamb, then lightly score the surface fat in a criss-cross pattern. Mix the sweet and smoked paprika with the ground ginger and a pinch each of salt and pepper. Rub all over the lamb, including the boned-out cavity, with a little olive oil. Place the lamb on a rack over a large roasting pan and stuff the boned cavity with the garlic cloves and half the orange slices. Pour a splash of water into the roasting pan.

Roast the lamb in the hot oven for 20 minutes, then reduce the oven temperature to 190°C/Gas 5 and roast for a further 20 minutes per 500g for pink lamb. If the top appears to be darkening too quickly during roasting, cover with foil. About 30 minutes before you calculate the lamb will be ready, lay the remaining orange slices over the meat.

Transfer the lamb to a warm platter, cover loosely with foil and leave to rest in a warm place for 10 minutes before carving.

When ready to serve, carve the lamb into thin slices and serve with new potatoes and a leafy salad.

1 part-boned leg of lamb, about
  2.4kg, knuckle bone left in
1 tsp sweet paprika
1 tsp smoked paprika
1 tsp ground ginger
sea salt and black pepper
little drizzle of olive oil
4–5 garlic cloves, halved, with
  skins left on
2 oranges, sliced

glazed gammon with
PINEAPPLE SALSA

SERVES 6

Drain the gammon and place in a large cooking pot. Cover with fresh water, bring to the boil and allow to bubble gently for 5–10 minutes. Skim off the scum and froth that rise to the surface, then pour off the water and re-cover the joint with fresh cold water. Bring to the boil, skim, then reduce the heat to a simmer and add the vegetables, herbs and peppercorns. Simmer for about 2 hours, checking the liquid from time to time and topping up with hot water as necessary.

Lift the gammon out of the pot onto a chopping board and leave to cool slightly. (If the liquor is not too salty, save it to make a pea and ham soup.) While still warm, cut away and discard the skin and most of the fat, leaving an even layer. Score lightly in a criss-cross pattern, then stud a clove in the middle of each scored diamond.

Heat the oven to 190°C/Gas 5. Place the gammon in a lightly oiled roasting pan. Mix together the marmalade, ginger, soy sauce and 2–3 tbsp of water to make a glaze and brush all over the gammon to coat evenly. Roast for 20–25 minutes, basting several times, until browned and nicely glazed. You may need to turn the pan around halfway through to ensure that the joint colours evenly.

Meanwhile, make the salsa. Cut away the peel and 'eyes' from the pineapple, then slice and remove the core. Cut into 1cm cubes and place in a large bowl. Peel the cucumber, halve lengthways and scoop out the seeds, then finely dice the flesh. Add to the pineapple with all the other ingredients and mix well. Let stand for at least 20 minutes.

Cover the cooked gammon with foil and allow to rest in a warm place for 15 minutes. Carve into thin slices and serve with the pineapple salsa and vegetables of your choice.

1 unsmoked boned gammon
  joint, about 2.6kg,
  soaked overnight
1 large carrot, peeled and cut into
  3 chunks
1 large onion, peeled and halved
2 large celery sticks, cut into
  3 chunks
1 bay leaf
few thyme sprigs
1 tsp black peppercorns
30–40 cloves
a little vegetable oil
3 tbsp marmalade
3cm knob of fresh root ginger,
  peeled and finely grated
2 tbsp light soy sauce

For the pineapple salsa
1 large ripe pineapple
1 small cucumber
1 red chilli, finely chopped
handful of coriander, leaves only,
  finely chopped
handful of mint, leaves only,
  finely chopped
sea salt and black pepper
1 tbsp sesame oil
2 tbsp olive oil
few dashes of Tabasco sauce
juice of ½ lemon

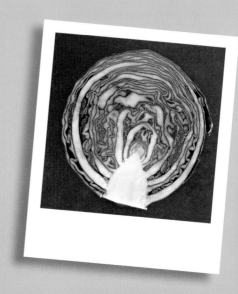

healthy
BARBECUES

squid, roast peppers
& CANNELLINI BEANS

SERVES 4

To prepare the squid, cut along one side of the body pouches to open them out, then lightly score the flesh in a criss-cross pattern. Lay the scored squid and tentacles in a wide, shallow dish and sprinkle with the herb leaves, coriander seeds, chilli, garlic, lemon zest and the juice of 1 lemon. Drizzle over the olive oil and toss the squid to coat all over with the marinade. Cover with cling film and leave to marinate in the fridge for 20–30 minutes.

Heat the barbecue or a griddle pan. Transfer the squid to a plate, ready to cook, scraping off and reserving the excess marinade.

Pat the roasted peppers with kitchen paper to absorb excess oil, then slice into strips. Heat the reserved marinade from the squid in a sauté pan and add the peppers, beans, remaining lemon juice and some seasoning. Sauté for 3–5 minutes to heat through. Set aside.

Place the squid on the barbecue or griddle pan, laying the scored pieces flat. Cook until the squid turns opaque, about 1 minute on each side for the scored pieces, a little longer for the tentacles. Remove to a plate. When cool enough to handle, slice the squid body into strips and cut the tentacles in half.

Stir the sliced squid and chopped parsley through the warm peppers and beans. Serve immediately.

3 large squid, about 180g each, cleaned, with tentacles
few thyme sprigs, leaves stripped
few rosemary sprigs, needles stripped
½ tsp coriander seeds, lightly crushed
1 small red chilli, sliced on the diagonal
2 garlic cloves, peeled and sliced
finely pared zest of 1 lemon
juice of 1½ lemons
2–3 tbsp olive oil
280g jar roasted peppers, drained
2 x 400g cans cannellini beans, drained and rinsed
sea salt and black pepper
small bunch of flat leaf parsley, leaves only, chopped

tandoori poussins
WITH MANGO RELISH

SERVES 4

To spatchcock the poussins, hold one, breast side down, on a chopping board. Using a pair of kitchen scissors, snip along both sides of the backbone to remove it. Turn the poussin over and press firmly down the middle with your hand to flatten it. Cut off the wing tips and trim off excess skin and fat. Repeat with the remaining birds.

For the marinade, mix all the ingredients together in a large shallow bowl. Add the poussins and turn them over so that each bird is well coated. Cover with cling film and leave to marinate in the fridge for several hours, or preferably overnight.

Heat the oven to 170°C/Gas 3. Transfer the poussins to a large baking tray, pour on the marinade from the bowl and sprinkle with some salt and pepper. Cover with foil and bake for 30–40 minutes until just cooked through. To test, prick the thickest part of each poussin with a skewer and press gently; the juices should run clear. Take off the foil and set aside to cool.

Meanwhile, make the mango relish. Peel the mango and chop the flesh, discarding the stone. Place in a bowl with the onion, chilli and lime juice. Toss to mix and season with salt and pepper to taste. Cover with cling film and chill for 20 minutes.

Heat the barbecue or a griddle pan until hot. Cook the poussins for 8–10 minutes, turning halfway, until nicely charred on both sides. Rest for a few minutes before serving, with the mango relish.

4 poussins, about 400–500g each

For the tandoori marinade
1 tsp ground turmeric
2 tsp garam masala
1 tsp ground coriander
1 tsp ground cumin
1 large garlic clove, peeled
    and crushed
3cm knob of fresh root ginger,
    peeled and finely grated
juice of ½ lemon
100ml natural yoghurt
small handful of coriander stalks,
    finely chopped
sea salt and black pepper

For the mango relish
1 ripe-but-firm mango
1 large red onion, peeled and
    finely chopped
1 red chilli, deseeded and
    finely chopped
juice of ½ lime

beef burgers with raita
& BEETROOT RELISH

SERVES 4

Put the minced beef into a large bowl and add the paprika, cayenne, ½ tsp salt (or less to taste) and ½ tsp pepper. Mix well with your hands, then shape into 4 neat patties. Place on a plate or tray, cover with cling film and chill for at least 30 minutes to set the shape.

Meanwhile, make the beetroot relish. Roughly chop the beetroot and place in a food processor with the capers, parsley, balsamic vinegar and olive oil. Pulse until the mixture is roughly chopped; you don't want to purée the beetroot. Season to taste and transfer to a bowl.

For the cucumber raita, peel the cucumber and quarter lengthways. Scrape out the seeds with a spoon and discard. Roughly chop the flesh and place in a bowl. Add the mint and toss with enough yoghurt to bind. Add the lemon juice and season with salt and pepper to taste.

Heat the barbecue, or heat a little olive oil in a non-stick frying pan. Brush the burgers with olive oil and cook on the barbecue, or pan-fry allowing 3½–4 minutes on each side for medium burgers. Remove to a warm plate and leave to rest for a few minutes. Add the tomatoes to the barbecue or pan and drizzle with olive oil and balsamic vinegar. Cook for 1–2 minutes until they are soft but still retain their shape.

Serve the burgers with the tomatoes, beetroot relish and cucumber raita. For a neat presentation, spoon the raita into Iceberg lettuce cups and garnish with a handful of rocket.

600g good-quality lean
  minced beef
1 tsp smoked paprika
pinch of cayenne pepper
sea salt and black pepper
olive oil, to cook and drizzle
250g cherry tomatoes on the vine
splash of balsamic vinegar
4 Iceberg lettuce leaves, trimmed
  to neaten (optional)
handful of wild rocket leaves
  (optional)

For the beetroot relish
250g cooked beetroot in natural
  juices, drained
3 tbsp capers, rinsed and drained
handful of flat-leaf parsley leaves,
  roughly chopped
2 tbsp balsamic vinegar
3 tbsp olive oil

For the cucumber raita
1 large cucumber
handful of mint leaves, chopped
3–4 tbsp natural yoghurt
squeeze of lemon juice, to taste

lamb kebabs with
PEPPERS & TOMATOES

SERVES 4

Cut the lamb steaks into 2.5cm cubes and place in a bowl. Stir together all the ingredients for the herb paste and pour over the lamb. Toss well to coat the pieces evenly. Cover with cling film and leave to marinate in the fridge for several hours, or overnight. When ready to cook, soak 6–8 bamboo skewers in cold water for least 20 minutes and return the lamb to room temperature.

Halve the peppers, remove the core and seeds, then cut into 2.5cm pieces. Thread the peppers, lamb, mushrooms and cherry tomatoes alternately onto the soaked skewers.

Heat the barbecue or place a griddle pan over a high heat. Drizzle a little olive oil over the skewers and sprinkle with some salt and pepper. Barbecue or grill the skewers for 2½–3 minutes on each side. Leave to rest for a minute or two, then serve with side salads of your choice.

500g lean lamb leg steaks
1 large red pepper
1 large yellow pepper
8 chestnut mushrooms
8 cherry tomatoes, skinned
   if preferred
olive oil, to drizzle

For the herb paste
finely grated zest and juice
   of 1 lemon
2 garlic cloves, peeled and
   finely chopped
½ tsp dried oregano
½ tsp dried mint
½ tsp dried thyme
¼ tsp dried ground rosemary
½ tsp dried tarragon
1 tbsp olive oil
sea salt and black pepper

four cabbage
COLESLAW

Cut out the core from each cabbage, then finely shred the leaves with a sharp knife. Place in a large bowl and toss well to mix.

For the dressing, whisk all the ingredients in a bowl, seasoning with salt and pepper to taste. Pour over the cabbage and toss to mix. Leave to marinate for at least 20 minutes.

Scatter the chives over the coleslaw and toss to mix just before serving.

¼ Chinese cabbage
¼ Savoy cabbage
¼ white cabbage
¼ red cabbage
handful of chives, finely snipped

For the dressing
3 tbsp extra-virgin olive oil
1 tbsp sesame oil
2 tbsp balsamic vinegar
2 tbsp wholegrain mustard
sea salt and black pepper

fennel, pea &
BROAD BEAN SALAD

SERVES 4

Trim the fennel, cutting off the base and removing the coarse outer layer of leaves. Cut each bulb in half lengthways, then slice as thinly as possible, using a mandolin or a sharp knife. Place in a large bowl of iced water and leave to soak for 10–15 minutes to crisp up.

Meanwhile, add the eggs to a pan of simmering water and simmer for 9 minutes (the yolks should be set but still quite soft). Immediately drain, then refresh in a pan of cold water.

Bring another pan of water to the boil. Add the broad beans and blanch for 1 minute, then add the peas and return to the boil. Blanch for another 3 minutes until the peas and broad beans are tender. Drain and refresh in a bowl of iced water.

For the dressing, whisk all the ingredients together in a bowl, seasoning with salt and pepper to taste.

Drain the fennel, broad beans and peas very well, and mix them in a large bowl. Pour over the dressing and toss. Shell the eggs, then cut into quarters lengthways.

When ready to serve, heat a tiny drizzle of olive oil in a non-stick pan and fry the Parma ham slices until golden brown and crisp, turning once. Divide the salad and eggs between serving plates. Break the crispy Parma ham into smaller pieces and scatter over the salads. Sprinkle with pepper and serve.

2 medium fennel bulbs
4 large eggs, at room temperature
250g podded broad beans
250g podded peas, thawed
   if frozen
olive oil, to drizzle
8 Parma ham slices

For the dressing
1 small garlic clove, peeled
   and crushed
1 tsp caster sugar, or to taste
1 tbsp lemon juice
1 tbsp wholegrain mustard
3 tbsp extra-virgin olive oil
handful of dill fronds,
   roughly chopped
sea salt and black pepper

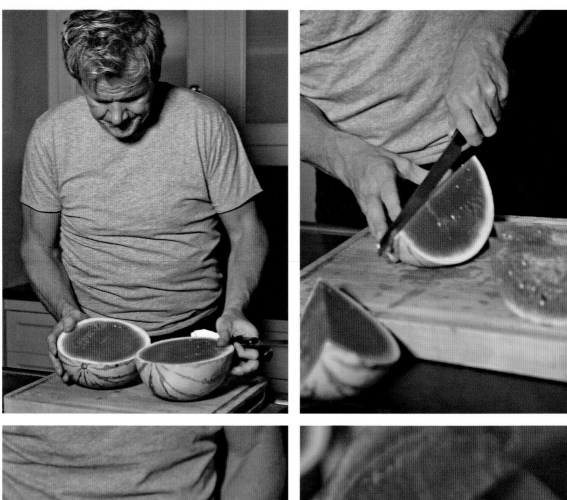

prawn, feta &
WATERMELON SALAD

SERVES 4

Marinate the prawns by tossing them together with 1 tbsp olive oil, a pinch of cayenne and some salt and pepper in a bowl. Cover with cling film and leave to marinate in the fridge for 10–15 minutes.

Cut the watermelon into wedges, then cut off the skin and slice the flesh thinly. Layer the watermelon slices on a large serving platter, interleaving them with rocket leaves. Crumble over the feta and grind over some black pepper.

Place a large, preferably non-stick frying pan over a medium heat and add the remaining olive oil. Tip in the prawns and fry for about 2 minutes until they turn opaque, turning them after a minute or so. Transfer to a plate and leave while you make the dressing.

Whisk the dressing ingredients together and season to taste. Add the prawns to the platter and scatter over the seeds, if using. Drizzle with the dressing and serve at once.

200g sustainably sourced raw
   prawns, peeled and deveined
2 tbsp olive oil
pinch of cayenne pepper
sea salt and black pepper
1.5kg ripe seedless watermelon
50g wild rocket leaves, washed
120g feta cheese
1 tbsp toasted mixed seeds, such
   as pumpkin and sunflower

For the dressing
2 tbsp lime juice
½ tsp caster sugar
4 tbsp extra virgin olive oil

root & leaf salad
WITH POMEGRANATE

SERVES 4

Trim the chicory, cutting off the base, then shred the leaves into matchsticks. Peel the carrots and cut them into ribbons, using a swivel vegetable peeler. Mix the chicory and carrot ribbons in a salad bowl. Roughly cut the beetroot into quarters and add to the bowl.

For the dressing, halve the pomegranate and scoop out the seeds and juice into a bowl, picking out and discarding any white, pithy membrane. Cut the orange in half and squeeze the juice into the bowl. Add the balsamic vinegar, olive oil and seasoning to taste. Blitz the mixture using a hand-held stick blender (or free-standing blender) until the pomegranate seeds are crushed. Pass the mixture through a fine nylon sieve, pressing down on the pulp with the back of a spoon.

Spoon the dressing over the salad (any extra will keep in the fridge for a few days). Scatter a handful of toasted hazelnuts over the salad to serve if you like.

3 heads of chicory
2 medium carrots
250g cooked beetroot in natural juices
handful of toasted hazelnuts, lightly crushed (optional)

For the dressing
1 pomegranate
1 orange
2 tbsp balsamic vinegar
3–4 tbsp extra virgin olive oil
sea salt and black pepper

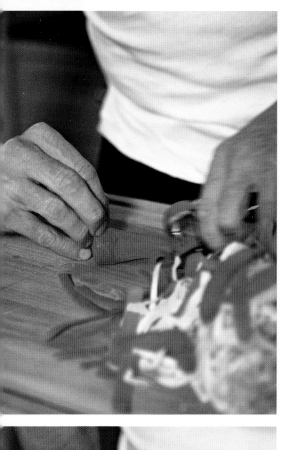

baked stuffed figs
WITH GOAT'S CHEESE

SERVES 4

Trim off the tip from each fig, then cut a cross through the top, cutting about halfway down. Squeeze the base of the figs to open out the top quarters like a flower.

Stuff the figs with the goat's cheese, sprinkle with chives and drizzle with balsamic vinegar. Scatter over the thyme leaves and pine nuts.

Stand the figs on a large piece of foil. Fold together the sides to seal the parcel. You can bake the figs in a preheated oven at 200°C/Gas 6, or on a barbecue. They should take 10–12 minutes. Unwrap the parcel and serve, as a starter, an accompaniment or to round off a meal.

8 ripe figs
100g soft goat's cheese
handful of chives, finely snipped
good-quality balsamic vinegar
few thyme sprigs, leaves stripped
2 tbsp toasted pine nuts

healthy
SUPPERS

fish cakes with
ANCHOVY DRESSING

SERVES 4

Peel the potatoes, cut into even-sized pieces and drop into a pan of well-salted water. Bring to the boil and cook for 10–15 minutes until tender when pierced with a knife. Drain well. While still hot, press the potatoes through a potato ricer back into the pan. Mix in the olive oil, lemon zest, lemon juice and seasoning to taste. Leave to cool.

Meanwhile, add the thyme, lemon slices and salmon to a wide pan of slowly simmering salted water and poach for a minute. Slide in the smoked haddock and gently poach for another 4–5 minutes until both fish are almost cooked through. Transfer to a plate, using a fish slice. When cool enough to handle, break the fish into large flakes, discarding the skin and any pin-bones.

Mix the fish and chopped herbs into the mashed potatoes, using your hands. Taste and adjust the seasoning. Divide the mixture into four and shape into neat patties. Season the flour with salt and pepper. Coat the fish cakes in seasoned flour, then dip into the egg and finally into the breadcrumbs, turning to coat evenly. Reshape them as necessary and place on a tray or plate. Chill for 2 hours to set the shape.

To cook, heat the oven to 180°C/Gas 4. Heat a thin layer of olive oil in a wide ovenproof frying pan. Fry the fish cakes for 2–3 minutes until golden brown, then flip over and fry the other side for 1–2 minutes. Finish cooking in the oven for 5–7 minutes.

Meanwhile, make the dressing, by gently warming all the ingredients together in a pan for 3–4 minutes. Spread a generous spoonful of dressing on each warm plate and rest a fish cake in the centre. Serve immediately, with peas or beans.

400g La Ratte, Charlotte or other waxy potatoes
sea salt and black pepper
2 tbsp olive oil, plus more to fry
finely grated zest of 1 large lemon
2–3 tbsp lemon juice
few thyme sprigs
½ lemon, sliced
300g sustainably sourced salmon fillet
300g sustainably sourced smoked haddock fillet
handful of flat leaf parsley leaves, chopped
handful of chervil leaves, chopped
3 tbsp plain flour
2 medium eggs, lightly beaten
50g Japanese panko breadcrumbs

For the anchovy dressing
2 tbsp capers, rinsed and drained
2 shallots, peeled and finely chopped
bunch of flat leaf parsley, leaves only, chopped
4 marinated anchovies, chopped
4 tbsp extra virgin olive oil

glazed ling with
SWEET-SOUR SHALLOTS

SERVES 4

Lay the fish fillets in a lightly oiled large baking dish and set aside.
Put the soy sauces, wine vinegar and sugar in a saucepan and stir
over a low heat to dissolve the sugar. Increase the heat and tip in the
coriander seeds, peppercorns and ginger. Boil for 8–10 minutes until
the liquid has reduced by half. Leave to cool completely.

Heat the oven to 180°C/Gas 4. Blanch the shallots in a pan of boiling
water for 10 minutes until tender, then drain.

Pour the soy mixture over the ling fillets and cook in the oven for
5 minutes until the sauce begins to caramelise. Scatter the blanched
shallots around the fish and pour on the white wine and fish stock.
Return to the oven and bake for another 6–8 minutes until the fish is
just cooked through.

Transfer the fish to a warm plate. Cover with foil and set aside in a
warm place for 5–10 minutes. Meanwhile, tip the onions and liquor
into a pan and boil for 10 minutes until reduced to a sticky sauce.

Place the fish on warm plates and spoon over the shallots and sauce.
Garnish with chives and serve with steamed rice and stir-fried pak
choi, if you wish.

NOTE If you are unable to find ling, you can use sustainably sourced
cod or whiting instead.

4 sustainably sourced skinless
    ling fillets, about 170g each
a little olive oil
4 tbsp light soy sauce
2 tbsp dark soy sauce
100ml white-wine vinegar
50g soft brown sugar
1 tsp coriander seeds, crushed
1 tsp black peppercorns, crushed
3cm knob of fresh root ginger,
    peeled and finely grated
400g small shallots, peeled
75ml dry white wine
150ml fish stock (see page 154)
small handful of chives, snipped

spiced monkfish with
MED POTATOES

Heat the oven to 200°C/Gas 6.

To cook the potatoes, add them to a pan of well-salted boiling water and cook for 10–15 minutes until tender.

Lay the monkfish on a board and remove any greyish membrane. Mix the five-spice powder, paprika and salt together on a plate. Roll the monkfish fillets in the spice mixture to coat evenly all over. Place a roasting pan in the oven to heat up.

Heat the olive oil in a heavy-based frying pan and sear the monkfish fillets, in batches if necessary, for 1½–2 minutes on each side until golden brown all over. Transfer the monkfish to the hot roasting pan and bake for 8–10 minutes until just cooked through. When ready, remove from the oven, cover with foil and leave to rest for 5 minutes.

Drain the potatoes as soon as they are done and return to the pan. Lightly crush them with the back of a fork or a potato masher and mix in the extra virgin olive oil, lemon juice and some seasoning. Stir in the chopped peppers, olives and basil. Taste and adjust the seasoning.

Cut the fish into thick slices. Spoon the potatoes onto warm serving plates and arrange the monkfish on top. Sprinkle with the chopped parsley and serve at once, with lemon wedges and spinach or broccoli.

4 sustainably sourced monkfish
  tail fillets, skinned, about
  170g each
1 tsp five-spice powder
1 tsp sweet paprika
1 tsp salt
2 tbsp olive oil
handful of flat leaf parsley leaves,
  chopped
lemon wedges, to serve

For the potatoes
750g new potatoes, scraped clean
sea salt and black pepper
2 tbsp extra-virgin olive oil
squeeze of lemon juice
200g drained roasted peppers in
  oil (from a jar), chopped
75g pitted black olives, roughly
  chopped
handful of basil leaves, shredded

seared yellowfin tuna
WITH BLACK BEANS

SERVES 4

Cook the beans first. Drain, then tip into a large pan and add the thyme, bay leaf, onion and carrot. Pour in enough water to cover by 3–4cm. Bring to a simmer and cook for 40–50 minutes until the beans are soft. Fish out the herbs, carrot and onion and discard. Drain the beans and leave to cool.

Heat a frying pan and add 3 tbsp olive oil. Tip in the red onions and garlic and cook, stirring frequently, for 4–6 minutes until they begin to soften but not brown. Stir in the black beans and cook for a few minutes to warm through. Use a fork to roughly mash the beans in the pan or gently pound with the end of a rolling pin, leaving some whole for a varied texture. If the mixture looks dry, add another 1 tbsp olive oil and a splash of water, then mix through the spring onions, coriander and lemon juice. Season with salt and pepper to taste. Keep warm while you cook the tuna.

Season the tuna with salt and pepper and coat one side of the steaks with the crushed coriander seeds. Heat a frying pan, add the olive oil and pan-fry the steaks for 2 minutes on each side. Transfer to a warm plate, cover with foil and leave to rest for a few minutes.

Divide the beans between warm serving plates and lay the tuna steaks on top. Serve at once.

4 sustainably sourced yellowfin
   tuna steaks, about 200g each
   and 2cm thick
sea salt and black pepper
1 tsp coriander seeds, lightly
   crushed
1½–2 tbsp olive oil

For the black beans
200g black beans, soaked
   overnight
few thyme sprigs
1 bay leaf
1 onion, peeled and halved
1 carrot, peeled and cut into
   3 chunks
3–4 tbsp olive oil
2 red onions, peeled and
   finely chopped
1 garlic clove, peeled and
   finely chopped
6 spring onions, trimmed
   and finely sliced
handful of coriander leaves,
   chopped
juice of ½ lemon, or to taste

herby crayfish
& PRAWN PILAF

SERVES 4

Heat the oven to 190°C/Gas 5. Cut a greaseproof paper circle slightly larger than the diameter of a heavy-based ovenproof pan or a cast-iron casserole. Snip a small hole in the middle of the paper to act as a vent.

Heat the pan with the olive oil, then sauté the onions for 4–6 minutes until they begin to soften. Stir in the rice, lemon zest, thyme, garlic and some seasoning. Stir well to toast the rice for a couple of minutes. Pour in the hot fish stock and bring to the boil. Add the crayfish and quickly cover with the greaseproof paper. Transfer to the oven.

After 15 minutes, take the pan out of the oven, lift the greaseproof paper and scatter over the prawns. Re-cover with the greaseproof paper and return to the oven for 10 minutes until the rice is tender and the prawns are just cooked through and opaque. Remove from the oven and leave to stand for about 5 minutes before lifting off the paper.

Fork through the rice to distribute the shellfish evenly. Check the seasoning and stir in the chopped herbs. Serve at once.

2–3 tbsp olive oil
3 small or 2 large red onions, peeled and thinly sliced
250g basmati rice
finely pared zest of 2 lemons
few thyme sprigs
2 garlic cloves (unpeeled), lightly smashed
sea salt and black pepper
550ml hot fish stock (see page 154)
750g sustainably sourced live crayfish, washed
250g sustainably sourced large shell-on raw prawns
handful of chives, snipped
handful of basil leaves, finely sliced
handful of chervil leaves, roughly chopped

braised aubergines
SZECHUAN-STYLE

SERVES 4

Cut the aubergines into 1½cm slices, then halve each into half-moons.

For the sauce, mix all the ingredients in a small bowl and set aside.

Heat a large pan and add half the oil. Tip in the ginger, garlic, onion and chilli and stir-fry over a medium heat for 4–5 minutes until the onion begins to soften. Stir in the red pepper and cook for another minute before adding the remaining oil and the aubergine pieces. Season lightly and cook, turning frequently, for 3–4 minutes.

Give the sauce a stir and pour into the pan. Stir well, then reduce the heat to low. Simmer for 8–10 minutes or until the aubergines are just tender, giving the mixture a stir every now and then.

Transfer to a serving dish and scatter over the spring onions and sesame seeds. Serve with bowls of steamed rice or Oriental noodles.

2 medium aubergines, trimmed
4 tbsp sunflower oil
3cm knob of fresh root ginger, peeled and finely chopped
2 garlic cloves, peeled and finely chopped
1 large onion, peeled and roughly chopped
1 red chilli, trimmed, deseeded and finely chopped
1 red pepper, cored, deseeded and chopped
sea salt and black pepper
2 spring onions, trimmed and thinly sliced on the diagonal
1 tbsp toasted sesame seeds, to garnish

For the sauce
150ml vegetable or chicken stock (see pages 154–5)
2 tbsp light soy sauce
2 tbsp rice wine
2 tsp Worcestershire sauce
2 tsp caster sugar, or to taste
1½ tsp cornflour

spiced pork chops
WITH SWEET POTATOES

Cut off the rind and excess fat around the pork chops. Mix the chilli powder, paprika and some salt and pepper with the olive oil in a wide, non-reactive baking dish. Add the thyme, garlic, star anise and coriander seeds. Add the pork chops and turn to coat. Cover and leave to marinate for at least 30 minutes, or put in the fridge and leave overnight. Return the chops to room temperature before continuing.

Heat the oven to 180°C/Gas 4. Bake the pork chops, uncovered, for about 15 minutes until the meat is just firm when lightly pressed.

Meanwhile, bring a pan of salted water to the boil. Peel the sweet potatoes and cut into 1½cm slices. Add to the pan and cook for 7–8 minutes until almost tender when pierced with a skewer. (They should be slightly undercooked at this stage.) Drain and refresh under cold running water. Dice the potatoes; set aside.

When cooked, transfer the chops to a warm plate, cover with foil and rest in a warm place for 10 minutes. Squeeze out the soft garlic from the skins and return to the baking dish. Add the chilli, tip in the sweet potatoes and toss to mix. Season lightly and bake for 10 minutes, stirring once or twice, until the potatoes are tender.

Stir the coriander leaves through the sweet potatoes and spoon onto warm plates. Add a pork chop to each plate and serve.

4 pork loin chops with bone, about 300g each

½–1 tsp mild chilli powder, to taste

1 tsp sweet paprika

sea salt and black pepper

2 tbsp olive oil

few thyme sprigs

4 garlic cloves, unpeeled and lightly smashed

5–6 star anise, lightly smashed

1 tsp coriander seeds, lightly crushed

3 large sweet potatoes, about 350g

1 red chilli, trimmed, deseeded and finely chopped

bunch of coriander, leaves only, chopped

vietnamese beef
& NOODLE SOUP

SERVES 4

Trim the beef of any sinew, then slice as thinly as possible. Place in a bowl and add the ginger, garlic, some pepper and the sesame oil. Toss to mix, cover and leave to marinate in the fridge for 30–40 minutes.

For the broth, pour the beef stock into a large pan and add the rest of the ingredients with a little salt and pepper. Bring to the boil, lower the heat and simmer for about 30 minutes. Strain the broth into a clean pan, discarding the ginger and spices. Taste and adjust the seasoning.

Add the rice noodles to a large pan of boiling salted water and cook according to the packet instructions until tender, but still retaining a bite. Drain in a colander and immediately toss the noodles with a little sesame oil to prevent them from sticking.

Bring the broth to the boil and tip in the beef and bean sprouts. Simmer for just 30 seconds, then remove from the heat.

Divide the noodles among warm bowls and ladle the hot broth over them, dividing the beef and bean sprouts equally. Scatter over the spring onions, coriander and mint. Serve immediately, with lime wedges and dishes of hoisin and Vietnamese chilli sauces for dipping.

500g beef fillet
2.5cm knob of fresh root ginger, peeled and finely grated
1 large garlic clove, peeled and crushed
sea salt and black pepper
1 tbsp sesame oil, plus more to toss
200g dried thin rice noodles
150g bean sprouts
2–3 spring onions, trimmed and thinly sliced on the diagonal
small bunch of coriander, leaves only
small bunch of mint or Thai sweet basil, leaves only

For the broth
1.5 litres beef stock (see page 155)
4cm knob of fresh root ginger, peeled and thinly sliced
4 star anise
3 cloves
2 cinnamon sticks
1 cardamom pod, lightly crushed
2 tsp caster sugar, or to taste
3 tbsp fish sauce

To serve
lime wedges
hoisin sauce
Vietnamese chilli sauce

stuffed chicken breasts
SALTIMBOCCA

SERVES 4

Cut a deep slit along one side of each chicken breast, without slicing right through, then open it out like a book. On a clean chopping board, finely chop 4 sage leaves, then mix into the ricotta and season with salt and pepper to taste.

Lay two Parma ham slices on the board, overlapping them slightly. Put a whole sage leaf in the middle and lay an open chicken breast, slit side up, on top. Spoon a quarter of the ricotta mixture onto the middle of the chicken, then fold the sides together again, to enclose the filling. Now wrap the Parma ham slices around the stuffed chicken breast. Wrap in cling film. Repeat with the rest of the chicken breasts and chill for 1–2 hours to firm up slightly.

Heat the oven to 180°C/Gas 4 and place a roasting pan in the oven to heat up. Heat a heavy-based frying pan and add the olive oil. When hot, fry the Parma-wrapped chicken, in batches if necessary, for 2 minutes on each side until browned. Lay a few thyme sprigs on each chicken breast, then place in the hot roasting pan. Cook in the oven for 12–15 minutes, depending on size, or until the meat feels just firm when lightly pressed.

Rest the chicken, covered, in a warm place for 5–10 minutes. Slice each breast thickly on the diagonal and arrange on warm plates. Serve with steamed greens and light mashed potatoes or zesty couscous.

4 large chicken breasts, about
    170–200g each
8 sage leaves
5 heaped tbsp ricotta
sea salt and black pepper
8 Parma ham slices
1½ tbsp olive oil
handful of thyme sprigs

wild mushroom &
COURGETTE RISOTTO

SERVES 4

Heat the oven to 200°C/Gas 6 and line a large baking tray with foil. Halve the courgettes lengthways and score the flesh in a criss-cross pattern. Arrange cut side up on the tray. Season lightly and scatter over the garlic slices and basil leaves. Drizzle with olive oil and squeeze over a little lemon juice. Bake for 30–40 minutes until the courgettes are soft. Let them cool slightly, then roughly chop the flesh.

For the risotto, bring the stock to a simmer in a pan. Heat another medium saucepan and add 1 tbsp olive oil. Stir in the rice and cook, stirring, for a minute. Pour in the wine and let it bubble to reduce down until the pan is quite dry. Gradually add the stock, a ladleful at a time, stirring frequently. Let the rice absorb most of the stock in the pan before adding another ladleful.

When the rice is al dente, stir in the chopped courgettes and turn off the heat. Leave the risotto to stand for a few minutes.

Meanwhile, heat a wide frying pan and add 1–2 tbsp olive oil. Tip in the mushrooms, season and toss over a high heat for 3–4 minutes until they are golden brown and any moisture has been cooked off. Mix the mushrooms into the risotto, adding a more boiling stock if you prefer a 'wet' risotto. Stir in most of the Parmesan and adjust the seasoning.

Divide the risotto among warm plates and sprinkle over the remaining Parmesan to serve.

4 courgettes
sea salt and black pepper
2 large garlic cloves, peeled and
   thinly sliced
few basil sprigs, leaves only
2–3 tbsp olive oil, plus more
   for the courgettes
squeeze of lemon juice
550–600ml vegetable or chicken
   stock (see pages 154–5)
200g risotto rice such as Carnaroli,
   Arborio or Vialone Nano
100ml dry white wine
200g wild mushrooms, cleaned,
   and halved or sliced if large
2–3 tbsp finely grated Parmesan

penne
PRIMAVERA

SERVES 4

For the pasta, bring a pot of salted water to the boil. At the same time, bring a large pan of water (that will take a large steamer basket) to the boil ready to steam the vegetables. Put all the baby vegetables into your steamer and sprinkle over the thyme sprigs and a little salt.

Set the steamer over the pan of boiling water. Cover and steam for 6–8 minutes until the vegetables are just tender.

Meanwhile, add the pasta to the boiling salted water and cook until al dente, according to the packet instructions. Reserving a little water in the pan, drain the pasta into a colander, then tip back into the pan and immediately toss with the olive oil and lemon juice.

When cooked, add the vegetables to the pasta, discarding the thyme sprigs. Toss to mix and season well to taste. Mix through the shredded herbs and divide between warm serving plates. Serve as is, or with a sprinkling of grated Parmesan.

300g dried penne or other pasta
sea salt and black pepper
8–10 baby leeks, white parts only
4 baby fennel, trimmed
8 radishes, trimmed and halved
   lengthways
6 baby carrots, scrubbed
   or peeled
4 baby turnips, scrubbed
   and halved
4 baby courgettes, trimmed and
   thickly sliced on the diagonal
few thyme sprigs
3–4 tbsp extra virgin olive oil
juice of ½ lemon
handful of basil leaves, shredded
handful of mint leaves, shredded
3–4 tbsp freshly grated Parmesan,
   to serve (optional)

moroccan pumpkin
& BUTTERBEAN POT

SERVES 4

Remove the skin from the pumpkin, discard the seeds and roughly chop the flesh into 5cm cubes. Heat half the olive oil in a large saucepan and add the pumpkin, shallot, garlic and some seasoning. Stir over a high heat for 10 minutes until the pumpkin cubes are lightly caramelised and soft. Add the spices and stir over the heat for another couple of minutes.

Pour in the stock to cover the pumpkin and bring to a simmer. Cook for 10 minutes, then remove from the heat and leave to cool slightly. While still hot, purée the mixture in a blender until smooth and creamy. (You may need to do this in two batches.)

Return the purée to the pan and bring to a simmer. Tip in the butterbeans and chopped herbs. Place over a medium heat for 2–3 minutes until the beans are hot. Taste and adjust the seasoning.

Ladle the soup into warm bowls and add a spoonful of yoghurt. Serve with plenty of warm flatbreads.

NOTE For a lighter version of this soup, as illustrated, use one can of butterbeans rather than two.

1kg wedge of cooking pumpkin (about 750g prepared weight)
4 tbsp olive oil
1 banana shallot (or 3 regular ones), peeled and chopped
2 garlic cloves, peeled and finely chopped
sea salt and black pepper
1 tsp paprika
1 tsp ground ginger
1 tsp ground cumin
1 tsp ground turmeric
500–600ml hot vegetable or chicken stock (see page 154–5)
2 x 400g cans butterbeans, drained and rinsed
bunch of flat leaf parsley, leaves only, chopped
bunch of coriander, leaves only, chopped
4 tbsp natural or Greek yoghurt, to serve

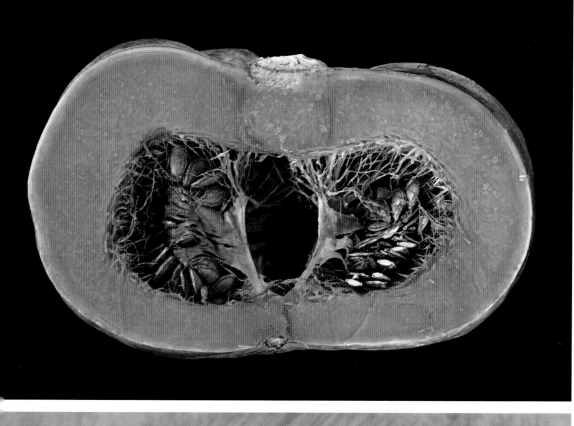

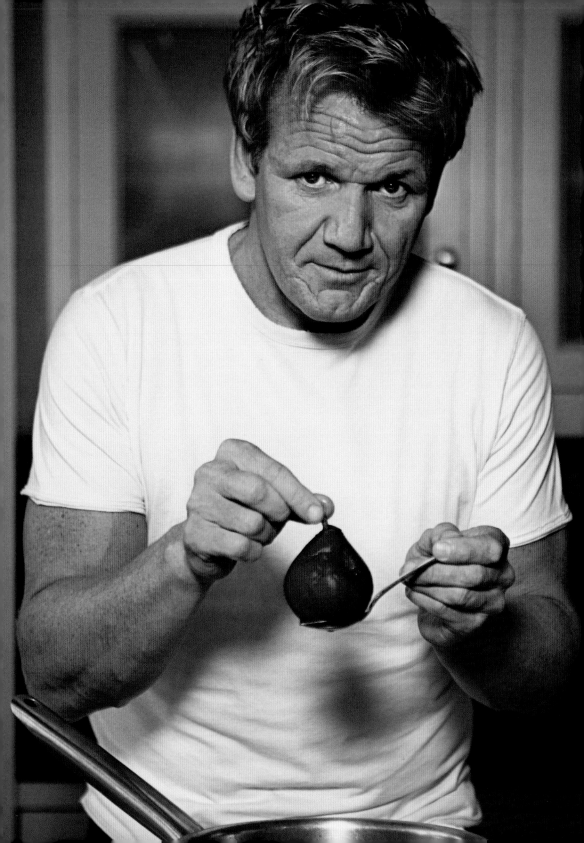

healthy
DESSERTS

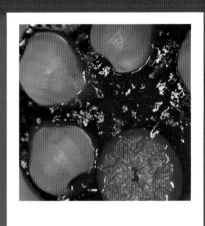

vanilla pannacotta
WITH BLUEBERRY SAUCE

SERVES 6

Pour the milk into a saucepan and scrape in the seeds from the vanilla pod, adding the pod too. Add the sugar and heat gently, stirring until the sugar has dissolved, then bring to a simmer. Meanwhile, soak the gelatine leaves in cold water for a few minutes to soften them.

As soon as the milk begins to bubble, remove the pan from the heat. Drain the gelatine leaves and squeeze out excess water, then add to the hot milk. Stir to dissolve, then leave to cool completely before straining through a fine sieve into a bowl.

Gradually add the cold milk to the yoghurt, stirring until completely combined. Pour the mixture into 6 pannacotta or dariole moulds and set them on a tray. Cover with a large piece of cling film and chill for a few hours, or overnight, until set.

For the sauce, put the blueberries, sugar and lemon juice into a saucepan. Bring to a simmer and cook for 3 minutes until the berries are soft, but not completely broken down. Transfer to a bowl and leave to cool, then chill.

To unmould each pannacotta, dip the mould in a bowl of warm water for a few seconds, then invert onto a plate and give it a gentle shake to release. If necessary, dilute the blueberry sauce with a tiny splash of water. Spoon a little sauce around each pannacotta and serve.

600ml whole or semi-skimmed milk
1 vanilla pod, split
125g caster sugar
4 sheets of leaf gelatine
200ml natural yoghurt

For the blueberry sauce
250g blueberries, rinsed and dried
3 tbsp caster sugar or honey
2–3 tbsp lemon juice

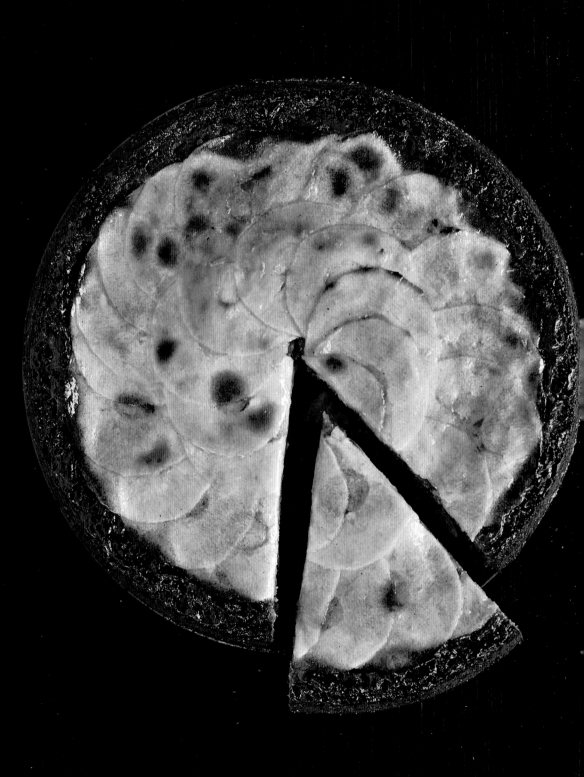

spiced apple
CAKE

SERVES 8

Peel, core and slice the cooking apples. Place in a wide pan with the sugar and butter. Cook over a high heat for 10–15 minutes, stirring often to prevent the apples from catching and burning, until the apples have become a pulp and any excess water has cooked off. Transfer to a bowl and cool completely. You should have about 475g purée.

Heat the oven to 170°C/Gas 3. Line and lightly butter a 23cm cake tin with a removable base. Peel, core and finely slice the eating apples, using a mandolin or sharp knife. Place in a bowl and pour over most of the lemon juice and a splash of water; set aside.

In a large bowl, mix together the wholemeal flour, baking powder, bicarbonate of soda, salt, sugar and ground spices. Make a well in the centre and add the egg, olive oil and apple purée. Fold into the dry ingredients until just combined.

Transfer the mixture to the prepared cake tin and gently level the top with a spatula. Bake the cake for 30 minutes until it feels just firm to the touch in the centre. Working quickly, overlap the sliced apples in concentric circles on top, leaving a margin around the edge. Brush the slices with a little of the remaining lemon juice and return to the oven for a further 30–35 minutes until a skewer inserted into the centre comes out clean.

Let the cake cool slightly before unmoulding onto a wire rack. Warm the apricot jam with 1–2 tbsp water, stirring until smooth. Brush over the top of the cake to glaze. Serve warm.

1kg cooking apples (5 or 6)
50g caster sugar
30g butter, plus more for the tin
2 ripe Braeburn or Cox's apples
juice of 1 lemon
225g wholemeal flour
1½ tsp baking powder
½ tsp bicarbonate of soda
¼ tsp fine sea salt
175g soft brown sugar
1 tsp ground cinnamon
1 tsp ground ginger
½ tsp freshly grated nutmeg
½ tsp ground cloves
1 large egg, lightly beaten
50ml light olive oil
2 tbsp apricot jam, to glaze

roast peaches with
SPICED VANILLA HONEY

SERVES 4

Heat the oven to 190°C/Gas 5. Cut the peaches in half and prise out the stones. Slice the peach halves into wedges and arrange on a non-stick baking tray. Add the spices and vanilla pod, then drizzle over the honey and peach liqueur.

Bake the peaches for 10–20 minutes until they are just tender and slightly caramelised around the edges. Remove from the oven and leave to cool slightly. Serve with a generous dollop of yoghurt, or spooned over very cold yoghurt sorbet (see page 149).

4–5 ripe-but-firm peaches
2 cinnamon sticks
2 star anise
1 vanilla pod, split
3–4 tbsp runny honey
generous splash of peach liqueur
    (or peach schnapps or brandy)
natural or Greek yoghurt,
    to serve

pavlova with
ROAST RHUBARB FOOL

Heat the oven to 140°C/Gas 1. Draw 6 circles, 8cm in diameter, on a sheet of silicone paper or baking parchment. Invert the paper onto an oiled baking sheet and lightly dust with cornflour. Mix the 1½ tsp of cornflour with 1 tbsp of the sugar in a small bowl and set aside.

Beat the egg whites in a clean, grease-free bowl to firm peaks, taking care not to over-whisk. Gradually beat in the remaining sugar, 1 tbsp at a time, and whisk until thick and glossy. Fold through the cornflour mixture, vanilla and vinegar.

Spoon the meringue into a large piping bag fitted with a 1–1½cm plain nozzle. Pipe concentric rounds over each circle to create a disc, then pipe two rings on the rim to form a shell. Bake for 40–45 minutes until dry and crisp. Turn off the oven and leave the meringues to cool slowly inside. (Ideally make them the evening before and leave to cool in the oven overnight.) Peel the meringues off the paper and store in an airtight container.

For the rhubarb, heat the oven to 200°C/Gas 6. Place the rhubarb in a lightly buttered roasting tin, sprinkle with the sugar and toss well. Roast for 15–20 minutes until tender. Tip the rhubarb and juices into a bowl, drizzle with honey and leave to cool completely.

To serve, ripple the roasted rhubarb and juices through the yoghurt to make a fool. Dust the meringue shells with a little icing sugar and place one on each serving plate. Spoon in the rhubarb fool and top with a mint sprig.

a little vegetable oil, for the tin
1½ tsp cornflour, plus 1 tsp more
    to dust
150g caster sugar
3 large egg whites (ideally from
    eggs about 1 week old)
1 tsp vanilla extract
½ tsp white-wine vinegar
icing sugar, to dust
mint sprigs, to finish

For the roast rhubarb fool
500g rhubarb, trimmed and
    roughly chopped
a little butter, for the tin
3–4 tbsp caster sugar
a little honey, to drizzle
400ml Greek yoghurt

poached pears
IN MULLED WINE

SERVES 4

Pour the red wine into a medium saucepan and add the sugar, spices, orange slices and stem ginger. Slowly bring to a simmer, stirring initially to dissolve the sugar. Simmer gently for 15–20 minutes to allow the aromatics to infuse their flavours into the wine.

Peel each pear, leaving the stalk on, and scoop out the core from the base with a melon baller. Gently lower the pears into the wine. Rest a crumpled piece of greaseproof paper with a small hole cut out in the centre on top; this will help to keep the pears submerged in the liquid.

Poach the pears for 10–20 minutes, depending on ripeness. To test, pierce with a metal skewer; it should meet little resistance. Transfer the pears and wine to a large bowl and leave to cool. Cover with cling film and refrigerate overnight to allow the flavours to develop.

Serve the pears warm, reheating gently, or at room temperature, with a scoop of vanilla ice cream or yoghurt sorbet (see page 149) if you like.

1 bottle of red wine
4 tbsp caster sugar
2 cinnamon sticks
½ tsp cloves
2 orange slices
1 globe of stem ginger in syrup, halved
4 ripe-but-firm pears, such as Williams

camomile-ginger jelly
WITH GINGER MELON

SERVES 4–6

Put the camomile tea, sugar and ginger into a warmed large teapot. Pour in 500ml of boiling water, put the lid on and leave to infuse for 4–5 minutes. Meanwhile, soak the gelatine leaves in cold water to cover for a few minutes to soften.

Strain the infused tea into a jug and discard the tea and ginger pieces. Drain and squeeze out the excess water from the gelatine, then add to the hot tea and stir to dissolve. Leave to cool completely. Pour into serving glasses and chill for 6 hours or longer until the jellies have set.

For the ginger melon, dissolve the sugar in 75ml of water in a small pan over a low heat, stirring occasionally. Increase the heat and bring to the boil, then add the ginger and simmer for 5 minutes. Remove from the heat and set aside to infuse until cold.

Cut the melon in half and remove the seeds. Scoop out the flesh into balls, using a melon baller, and place in a large bowl. Strain the infused syrup over the melon. Leave to macerate for 10 minutes.

To serve, spoon a few melon balls onto each jelly and drizzle with a little of the ginger syrup.

10g camomile loose leaf tea,
   or 2 camomile tea bags
85g caster sugar
finger length knob of fresh root
   ginger, thickly sliced
3 sheets of leaf gelatine

For the ginger melon
75g caster or granulated sugar
small knob of fresh root ginger,
   peeled, cut into matchsticks
1 Charentais, or a small
   honeydew melon

lime
MOUSSE

SERVES 8

Soak the gelatine leaves in cold water to cover for a few minutes to soften. Meanwhile, put the lime juice in a measuring jug and top up with cold water to reach 200ml. Pour into a saucepan and add half the sugar. Stir over a low heat to dissolve, then increase the heat and bring to a simmer. Take the pan off the heat.

Drain the gelatine leaves and squeeze out excess water, then add to the lime syrup and stir to dissolve. Leave to cool completely.

Beat the egg whites in a clean, grease-free bowl with an electric whisk until they form stiff peaks. Beat in the remaining sugar, 1 tbsp at a time, until fully incorporated and the meringue is firm.

In another bowl, lightly beat the crème fraîche, then stir in the cooled lime mixture. (The combination will be quite loose at this stage.) Fold in the meringue, then spoon into small serving glasses.

Chill the mousses for a few hours to firm up. Sprinkle over a little lime zest before serving.

2 sheets of leaf gelatine
juice of 4 limes (about 150ml)
175g caster sugar
2 medium egg whites
200ml reduced-fat crème fraîche
finely grated zest of 1–2 limes

orange & cinnamon
RICOTTA CHEESECAKE

SERVES 8

Heat the oven to 150°C/Gas 2. Lightly butter a deep 20cm cake tin with a removable base.

For the crust, break up the biscuits and whizz in a food processor to fine crumbs. Add the melted butter and pulse until the mixture comes together. Tip into the prepared tin and press down firmly with the back of a spoon to create a neat crust. Stand the tin on a baking sheet and bake for 10–12 minutes until lightly browned. As you remove it from the oven, brush the crust with the egg white to seal. Leave to cool slightly. Clean the processor.

For the ricotta filling, whizz all the ingredients in the food processor until well blended. (You may need to scrape down the sides once or twice.) Pour the filling over the crust and bake for 30 minutes until it has just set around the sides but is still quite runny in the middle.

Turn off the heat but leave the cheesecake in the oven to cool slowly; the filling will continue to set as it cools. Leave until completely cold, preferably overnight.

To prepare the oranges if serving, cut off the tops and bottoms and stand them upright on a board. Cut along the curve of the fruits to remove the skin and white pith, then slice into rounds, flicking out the seeds as you go, and place in a bowl. Heat a heavy-based frying pan until hot, add the sugar and let it caramelise over a high heat. Protecting your hand (as the mixture will splutter), add the liqueur and a splash of water. The caramel may harden, but it will return to a syrup as you stir over a low heat. Pour over the orange slices and toss.

To serve, run a knife around the cheesecake and unmould onto a plate. Serve with the oranges in syrup if desired.

For the biscuit crust
40g lightly salted butter, melted, plus more for the tin
150g reduced-fat digestive biscuits
1 egg white, lightly beaten

For the ricotta filling
500g ricotta cheese
250g quark
100g caster sugar
1 tbsp cornflour
3 large eggs
finely grated zest of 1 orange
2–3 tbsp Grand Marnier or Cointreau, to taste
½ tsp ground cinnamon

For the oranges in syrup (optional)
4 large navel oranges
50g caster sugar
60ml Grand Marnier or Cointreau

yoghurt
SORBET

Pour 350ml of water into a heavy-based pan, add the sugar and liquid glucose and place over a low heat. Stir occasionally until the sugar has dissolved, then increase the heat and boil for 3–4 minutes. Remove from the heat and cool completely.

Beat the yoghurt and fromage frais together in a bowl until smooth and creamy. Mix in the cooled syrup.

Pour the mixture into an ice-cream machine and churn until almost firm, then scoop the sorbet into a suitable container and freeze for several hours until firm. If you do not have an ice-cream machine, freeze the mixture in a shallow container and beat with a fork several times during freezing.

Delicious served with both hot and cold desserts, or scooped into glasses with fresh fruit.

VARIATIONS

Purée ½ ripe-but-firm mango and chop the other half. Fold the purée into the sorbet mixture before freezing; fold in the chopped mango halfway through churning.

Purée the flesh of 2–3 ripe, skinned nectarines or peaches until smooth and fold into the sorbet base before freezing.

Reduce the amount of water to 300ml. Add the finely grated zest and juice of 2 limes to the sorbet mixture before freezing. Serve with griddled pineapple wedges.

225g caster sugar
3 tbsp liquid glucose
300ml natural yoghurt
100ml fromage frais

chocolate
MOUSSE

SERVES 4

Melt the chocolate in a heatproof bowl set over a pan of simmering water (make sure the bowl does not touch the water). Meanwhile, put the honeycomb bars into the freezer for 10 minutes. When the chocolate has melted, remove from the heat and set aside.

For the meringue, put the sugar, liquid glucose and 2 tbsp of water into a saucepan and place over a low heat until the sugar has dissolved, stirring a couple of times. Increase the heat and boil the syrup until it registers 120°C on a sugar thermometer; this is called the 'hard ball stage', when a little of the hot syrup dropped into a glass of water hardens to a form a clear ball.

Meanwhile, beat the egg whites in a clean, grease-free bowl to stiff peaks. Still whisking, slowly trickle the hot syrup onto the egg whites. Continue to whisk until the egg whites are smooth, glossy and have tripled in volume. The sides of the bowl should no longer feel hot.

Add the crème fraîche to the melted chocolate and whisk to combine. Fold the chocolate mixture into the meringue, followed by the coffee liqueur if using.

Remove the wrapper from one of the chilled honeycomb bars and wrap in a clean tea towel. Place on a board and bash lightly with a rolling pin to crush the honeycomb. Open up the tea towel and tip the crushed honeycomb into the mousse, then gently fold it in.

Spoon the mousse into small serving dishes set on a tray. Grate over a layer of chocolate-coated honeycomb, followed by a layer of chocolate. Chill for a few hours before serving.

150g dark chocolate, in pieces, plus 25g more for grating
2 chocolate-coated honeycomb bars (Crunchie bars)
100g caster sugar
1 tsp liquid glucose
2 large egg whites
100ml crème fraîche
1–2 tbsp Kahlua or other coffee liqueur (optional)

healthy
BASICS

vegetable STOCK

MAKES ABOUT 1.5 LITRES

Put the vegetables, garlic, peppercorns and bay leaf in a large stockpot and pour on cold water to cover, about 2 litres. Bring to the boil, reduce the heat to a simmer and leave to cook gently for 20 minutes. Remove from the heat and add the bundle of herbs, white wine and a little seasoning. Give the stock a stir and leave to cool completely.

Chill the stock overnight before straining, if you have time. Pass through a fine sieve into a bowl. Refrigerate and use within 5 days, or freeze in smaller amounts for up to 3 months.

3 onions, peeled and
   roughly chopped
1 leek, washed and
   roughly chopped
2 celery sticks, roughly chopped
6 carrots, peeled and
   roughly chopped
1 head of garlic, halved crossways
1 tsp white peppercorns
1 bay leaf
few thyme, basil, tarragon,
   coriander and parsley sprigs,
   tied together
200ml dry white wine
sea salt and black pepper

fish STOCK

MAKES ABOUT 1.5 LITRES

Heat the olive oil in a stockpot and add the onion, celery, fennel and a little seasoning. Stir over a medium heat for 3–4 minutes until the vegetables begin to soften but not brown. Add the fish bones and trimmings and the wine, then pour in cold water to cover. Simmer for 20 minutes, then remove from the heat and leave to cool.

Ladle the stock through a fine sieve into a bowl and discard the solids. Refrigerate and use within 2 days, or freeze in smaller amounts for up to 3 months.

2 tbsp olive oil
1 small onion, peeled and
   roughly chopped
½ celery stick, roughly sliced
1 small fennel bulb,
   roughly chopped
sea salt and black pepper
1kg white fish bones and trimmings
   (or crab or lobster shells)
75ml dry white wine

chicken STOCK

Heat the olive oil in a large stockpot and add the vegetables, herbs and garlic. Cook over a medium heat, stirring occasionally, until the vegetables are golden. Stir in the tomato purée and flour and cook for another minute. Add the chicken bones, then pour in cold water to cover. Season lightly. Bring to the boil and skim off any scum that rises to the surface. Reduce the heat and leave to simmer gently for 1 hour.

Let the stock stand for a few minutes, then pass through a fine sieve and leave to cool. Refrigerate and use within 5 days, or freeze in smaller amounts for up to 3 months.

2 tbsp olive oil
1 carrot, peeled and
  roughly chopped
1 onion, peeled and
  roughly chopped
2 celery sticks, roughly chopped
1 leek, washed and roughly sliced
1 bay leaf
1 thyme sprig
3 garlic cloves, peeled
2 tbsp tomato purée
2 tbsp plain flour
1kg raw chicken bones
sea salt and black pepper

beef STOCK

Heat the oven to 220°C/Gas 7. Put the bones in a roasting tray and drizzle with a little olive oil. Roast for about 1 hour, turning over halfway, until evenly browned. Meanwhile, cut the onions, carrots, celery and fennel into rough 5cm chunks.

Heat the 2 tbsp of olive oil in a large stockpot and add the vegetables. Cook, stirring frequently, over a high heat until golden brown. Stir in the tomato purée and cook for another 2 minutes. Add the browned bones and pour in cold water (about 2–2.5 litres) to cover. Bring to a simmer and skim off the froth and scum that rise to the surface. Add the mushrooms, herbs and peppercorns. Simmer for 6–8 hours until the stock has a deep, rich flavour.

Leave to stand for a few minutes, then pass the stock through a fine sieve. Leave to cool, then refrigerate and use within 5 days, or freeze in smaller amounts for up to 3 months.

1.5 kg beef or veal marrow bones,
  chopped into 5–6cm pieces
2 tbsp olive oil, plus more for
  the bones
2 onions, peeled
2 carrots, peeled
2 celery stalks, peeled
1 large fennel bulb, trimmed
1 tbsp tomato purée
100g button mushrooms
1 bay leaf
1 thyme sprig
1 tsp black peppercorns

INDEX

P

pancakes: buckwheat pancakes with smoked salmon 15

pannacotta with blueberry sauce 134

paprika: roast lamb with paprika & oranges 85

Parma ham: devilled caesar salad with Parma ham 36

   fennel, pea & broad bean salad 100

   stuffed chicken breasts saltimbocca 124

pasta: penne primavera 128

   spaghetti vongole 45

pavlova with roast rhubarb fool 141

peaches: roast peaches with spiced vanilla honey 138

pears: poached pears in mulled wine 142

peas: baked sea bass with lemon couscous 68

   fennel, pea & broad bean salad 100

penne primavera 128

peppers: braised aubergines Szechuan-style 120

   lamb kebabs with peppers & tomatoes 96

   spiced monkfish with Med potatoes 115

   squid, roast peppers & cannellini beans 90

   Thai rice noodle salad with prawns 57

Persian-style onion soup 33

pheasant & ginger casserole 77

pies: venison pie with sweet potato topping 82

pilaf, herby crayfish & prawn 118

pineapple salsa, glazed gammon with 86

poached pears in mulled wine 142

pomegranate: pomegranate & banana smoothie 25

   root and leaf salad with pomegranate 104

pork: spiced pork chops with sweet potatoes 121

porridge 13

potatoes: fish cakes with anchovy dressing 111

   spiced monkfish with Med potatoes 115

   venison pie with sweet potato topping 82

poussins: tandoori poussins with mango relish 93

prawns: herby crayfish & prawn pilaf 118

   prawn, feta & watermelon salad 103

   Thai rice noodle salad with prawns 57

pumpkin: Moroccan pumpkin & butterbean pot 130

Q

quark: orange & cinnamon ricotta cheesecake 148

R

radishes: glazed salmon with spinach-radish salad 62

   penne primavera 128

raita, cucumber 95

raspberries: berry & yoghurt smoothie 25

relishes: beetroot relish 95

   mango relish 93

rhubarb: pavlova with roast rhubarb fool 141

rice: herby crayfish & prawn pilaf 118

   warm ham hocks with wild rice & basmati 39

   wild mushroom & courgette risotto 127

ricotta: orange & cinnamon ricotta cheesecake 148

   stuffed chicken breasts saltimbocca 124

   ricotta & walnut baked mushrooms 22

risotto, wild mushroom & courgette 127

rocket: prawn, feta & watermelon salad 103

   smoked trout, orange & wild rocket salad 35

root & leaf salad with pomegranate 104

S

salads: devilled caesar salad with Parma ham 36

   fennel, pea & broad bean salad 100

   flatbread, feta & chickpea salad 58

   four cabbage coleslaw 99

   glazed salmon with spinach-radish salad 62

   mango, avocado & smoked chicken salad 65

   melon & berry salad 10

   prawn, feta & watermelon salad 103

   root & leaf salad with pomegranate 104

   smoked trout, orange & wild rocket salad 35

   Thai rice noodle salad with prawns 57

   warm ham hocks with wild rice & basmati 39

salmon: fish cakes with anchovy dressing 111

   see also smoked salmon

salsas: pineapple salsa 86

   tomato salsa 41

sea bass: baked sea bass with lemon couscous 68

shallots: glazed ling with sweet-sour shallots 112

shiitake mushrooms: soba noodle soup with chicken & shiitake 47

smoked haddock: fish cakes with anchovy dressing 111

smoked salmon: buckwheat pancakes with smoked salmon 15

   glazed salmon with spinach-radish salad 62

smoked trout, orange & wild rocket salad 35

smoothies: berry & yoghurt smoothie 25

   fig, honey & yoghurt smoothie 25

   pomegranate & banana smoothie 25

soba noodle soup with chicken & shiitake 47

sorbet, yoghurt 149

soufflé, spinach & goat's cheese 42

soups: borlotti bean minestrone 55

   borscht 51

   chilled watercress & spinach soup 52

   cod & tomato chowder 30

   Moroccan pumpkin & butterbean pot 130

Persian-style onion soup 33

   soba noodle soup with chicken & shiitake 47

Once more, I am indebted to my marvellous team who time and again astound me with their creativity and commitment. Specifically, my special thanks to Mark Sargeant; Emily Quah for brilliantly ensuring that the recipes are mouth-wateringly delicious and healthy; Helen Lewis for making the book look so smart and beautiful; Lisa Barber for her great photography; Janet Illsley for her amazing editorial thoroughness; Nicola for her intensive work on the layouts; and Anne Furniss and Alison Cathie at Quadrille for their continual support. Also to Pat Llewellyn and her team at Optomen for producing a fantastic series; and everyone who keeps the business running smoothly while we focus on producing great food, books and television; finally to my talented wife, Tana.